Family Activities

101 Fun Ideas, Games, and Crafts to Strengthen Parent-Child Relationships

© Copyright 2024 - All rights reserved.

The content contained within this book may not be reproduced, duplicated, or transmitted without direct written permission from the author or the publisher.

Under no circumstances will any blame or legal responsibility be held against the publisher or author for any damages, reparation, or monetary loss due to the information contained within this book, either directly or indirectly.

Legal Notice:

This book is copyright-protected. It is only for personal use. You cannot amend, distribute, sell, use, quote, or paraphrase any part of the content within this book without the consent of the author or publisher.

Disclaimer Notice:

Please note the information contained within this document is for educational and entertainment purposes only. All effort has been executed to present accurate, up-to-date, reliable, and complete information. No warranties of any kind are declared or implied. Readers acknowledge that the author is not engaging in the rendering of legal, financial, medical, or professional advice. The content within this book has been derived from various sources. Please consult a licensed professional before attempting any techniques outlined in this book.

By reading this document, the reader agrees that under no circumstances is the author responsible for any losses, direct or indirect, that are incurred as a result of the use of the information contained within this document, including, but not limited to, errors, omissions, or inaccuracies.

Table of Contents

INTRODUCTION 1
CHAPTER 1: THE IMPORTANCE OF BUILDING BONDS 2
CHAPTER 2: SCREEN-FREE ACTIVITIES 8
CHAPTER 3: OUTDOOR ADVENTURE IDEAS 30
CHAPTER 4: CREATIVE SOULS: UNLEASH YOUR INNER ARTISTS 45
CHAPTER 5: REVAMPING GAME NIGHT 54
CHAPTER 6: COOKING AND BAKING AS A FAMILY 60
CHAPTER 7: SHARING AND CREATING STORIES 68
CHAPTER 8: ACTIVITIES FOR FITNESS AND FUN 75
CHAPTER 9: TRAVELING TOGETHER: DAY TRIP IDEAS 86
CHAPTER 10: CELEBRATING TOGETHERNESS: FAMILY TRADITIONS TO CHERISH 91
CONCLUSION 94
CHECK OUT ANOTHER BOOK IN THE SERIES 95
REFERENCES 96

Introduction

Spending quality time with family is crucial and adds meaning to our lives. Unfortunately, with busy schedules and daily routines, we often forget to make time for our loved ones. So, developing activities to bond the family and create lasting memories becomes vital. This comprehensive guide shares some fun ideas for family activities to keep everyone entertained.

Spending quality time with family strengthens relationships. These bonds create and nurture the relationship between family members, making them feel close to one another. Taking part in activities together is an excellent way to do this. This book also includes ideas for screen-free games and projects so you can talk, laugh, and share stories as a family. It also covers tasks that encourage teamwork and create a sense of unity in the family.

In today's world, screens dominate our lives, and it's no secret that excessive screen time can damage the bond between family members. While technology can be helpful, taking a break from screens and finding other ways to spend quality time together is vital. Hidden in the pages of this book are outdoor adventure ideas that can help the family reconnect with nature.

Creative souls will get to unleash their inner artists when they explore the art and craft ideas included in this book. Game night can also be exciting with some interesting twists, which will be discussed in later chapters. Cooking together is a great way to bond and learn from each other. So, why not put on aprons and get everyone to spend time in the kitchen? Baking is another activity that will bring the family together with a yummy result.

Storytelling is a powerful tool used for centuries as an ancient form of entertainment. This guide will teach you to share stories and make tales together, creating a magical atmosphere. Fitness activities have also been added for those who want to stay active together as a family. Finally, explore some ideas for day trips you can take together and create wonderful, lasting memories with your loved ones. This book also includes ideas for family traditions you can start and cherish forever.

Spending quality time with your family should be a smooth process. With this guide, you will find many fun activities the whole family can enjoy together. Regardless of where you are or what you're doing, setting aside some time for your family is essential. After all, the family is all we have when it comes down to it. So why not use this book as a starting point and create some fantastic memories together? Happy bonding!

Chapter 1: The Importance of Building Bonds

To foster strong, positive relationships between parents and their children, the time you spend together has to be of high quality. Whether enjoying a stroll around the park or playing board games together, engaging in fun activities with your family is a sure way to build lasting bonds. This chapter examines the importance of precious quality family time and its impact on parent-child relationships, how flexibility in activities can lead to greater connection and the educational benefits of engaging in fun activities together. You'll also find some tips and tricks on fostering a stronger, more meaningful relationship between parents and their children.

Quality Time and Its Impact on Parent-Child Relationships

Spending quality time with your children can help you build a healthy parent-child relationship.
https://unsplash.com/photos/VJVsEnR_vNE?utm_source=unsplash&utm_medium=referral&utm_content=creditShareLink

Spending dedicated quality time with your child is essential to building a strong and healthy parent-child relationship. Quality time means giving undivided attention to your family, communicating clearly, listening actively, participating in activities together, and creating precious memories. This section will explore the importance of quality time, explain how it impacts parent-child relationships, and suggest ways to incorporate it into your daily routine.

Importance of Quality Time

Quality time is one of the keys to building a close, supportive, and long-lasting relationship with your child. Children feel loved and valued when they receive attention and affection from their parents. When parents devote time to their children, they establish a strong bond and trust that can improve communication, reduce negative behavior, and promote emotional and social development. In addition, quality time builds confidence, self-esteem, and a sense of security in children, making them better able to cope with challenges and stress in the future.

Impact of Quality Time on Parent-Child Relationships

Spending regular quality time with your child helps you understand your child's needs, interests, strengths, and weaknesses. It deepens your connection and trust with your child, leading to better communication, problem-solving, and decision-making. Research has shown that children with quality time with their parents are less likely to experience depression, anxiety, and behavioral problems. In addition, they are more likely to perform better academically, have better social skills, and be less likely to engage in risky behaviors, such as drug and alcohol abuse.

Ways to Incorporate Quality Time into Your Daily Routine

You don't have to spend hours to provide quality time for your child. Instead, you can incorporate quality time into your daily routine, even with a busy schedule. Here are some ideas:

- **Create a Family Ritual.** For example, have dinner together every night, read a book before bedtime, or go on a weekend outing.
- **Turn Off Distractions.** Be fully present when spending time with your child. Turn off your phone, the TV, or anything distracting.
- **Ask Open-Ended Questions.** Encourage conversation by asking open-ended questions like "What was the best part of your day?" or "Tell me about your favorite hobby."
- **Participate in Your Child's Interests.** Join your child in activities that interest them, such as playing board games, drawing, or sports.
- **Plan One-on-One Time:** Plan special activities or outings with each child. It could be as simple as going for a walk or baking cookies.

Quality Time Is Not Just for Children

Quality time is not just for children but for parents, too. Spending time with your child can help you relax, reduce stress, boost your mood, and improve your mental health. It is also an opportunity to learn from your child, have fun, and create memories that will last a lifetime. As a parent, it can be easy to put yourself last, but remember, self-care is as important as taking care of your child. Make sure you have time to recharge, reflect, and appreciate the joys of parenting.

Spending quality time with your child is a valuable investment in your child's life and well-being. It is an opportunity to build a solid and lasting parent-child relationship, promote your child's emotional and social development, and create precious memories. Remember, quality time does not have to be complicated or expensive. It can be as simple as reading a book or having a conversation. Make time for your child, turn off distractions, and enjoy each other's company. Your child will thank you for it.

The Power of Flexibility in Parent-Child Relationships

Parenting can be challenging and sometimes frustrating, especially when we do not have all the answers. But we need to understand that our children are not robots. Instead, they are unique individuals with their own particular personalities, strengths, and weaknesses. Therefore, adopting a flexible parenting style that can adapt to your children's different needs and developmental stages is crucial. This section will explore the power of flexibility in parent-child relationships and its impact on your children's overall well-being.

Accepting your child's individuality is a big step in exercising flexibility.
https://pixabay.com/id/photos/gadis-ibu-anak-perempuan-2480361/

    The first step to implementing flexibility is understanding and accepting our child's individuality. Every child has a different temperament, learning style, and pace. So, a one-size-fits-all approach is not going to work. Instead, we should focus on adapting our parenting to fit each child's individual needs. By embracing your child's individuality, you create a nurturing environment that supports their emotional and psychological development.

Scientific Benefits of Engaging in Fun Activities with the Family

Doing fun activities as a family has many scientific benefits.
https://www.pexels.com/photo/family-playing-charades-at-bonfire-in-garden-5638830/

Family time is crucial in today's fast-paced world, where everyone is busy. Spending quality time with family strengthens bonds and has numerous benefits, such as reducing stress levels, boosting self-esteem, and improving mental health. What's even more interesting is engaging in fun activities as a family can lead to significant scientific benefits that impact our lives in both short-term and long-term ways. Let's explore some of these surprising scientific benefits of engaging in fun activities with family:

- **Improved Cognitive Functioning:** Family fun activities involving games, sports, or puzzles can enhance cognitive processes, such as memory, reasoning, and problem-solving skills. Studies reveal that family fun activities boost creativity and improve mental resilience, enhancing brain connectivity and overall cognitive functioning.
- **Better Emotional Stability:** Engaging in fun activities with family regulates mood and reduces stress levels. Family fun time develops a sense of belonging and emotional security, contributing to stable emotional health. In addition, studies suggest that family fun time provides emotional support and strengthens empathy and compassion in children.
- **Healthy Physical Development:** Activities, such as outdoor sports, hiking, or cycling all improve physical development and lead to healthier lifestyles. Engaging in fun physical activities with family promotes physical exercise, leading to better cardiovascular health, stronger bones, enhanced muscle strength, and a better immune system.
- **Improved Communication Skills:** Engaging in family activities opens up opportunities for family members to communicate and interact in a relaxed, non-judgmental setting. This

develops better communication skills, leading to enhanced social functioning and improved relational dynamics within the family.
- **Long-Term Social Benefits:** Engaging in fun activities has long-term social benefits too. Positive family experiences lead to better academic performance, improved social functioning, and improved relationships with peers later in their lives.

Engaging in fun activities with family strengthens family bonds and has several surprising scientific benefits. These benefits impact our lives in both short and long-term ways, contributing to better cognitive functioning, healthier physical development, improved emotional stability, and better communication skills.

Tips for Fostering Family Connections

Family is the most important thing in everyone's life. It's the foundation of our support, love, and care. However, spending quality time with our families with our busy lives and schedules can be challenging. This section will discuss tips that will help you foster stronger family connections, regardless of your busy life.

- **Set Aside Time for Family:** The first step to cultivating family connections is to set aside time for family. No matter how busy your schedule is, prioritize spending time with your loved ones. It can be done by planning family outings, game nights, or simply sitting down for dinner together. When you set aside time for family, you make it clear that they are a priority in your life, which builds more robust connections.
- **Create Shared Experiences:** Shared experiences are a great way to build stronger connections with family members. It can be anything from going on a vacation, taking a cooking class, or simply trying out a new hobby together. The key is finding something you all enjoy, allowing you to get closer over a common interest. It not only creates lasting memories but also strengthens the family bond.
- **Communicate Regularly:** Communication is vital to building strong family connections. Always check in with your family and ask about their day-to-day life. This can be done by simply sending a text or making a quick phone call. By staying connected and engaging in open communication, you can better understand each other's thoughts and feelings, strengthening your relationship.
- **Be Present Now:** Being present is essential when spending time with family. This means putting away distractions like your phone and focusing on the present moment. You can strengthen your bond and create lasting memories by giving your undivided attention.

In conclusion, family connections are essential to our well-being, and it's vital to make an effort to strengthen them. By setting aside time for family, creating shared experiences, communicating regularly, practicing forgiveness, and being present in the moment, you can foster stronger family connections that will last a lifetime. Love and support begin with family, so make the most of it.

Fostering Strong Parent-Child Relationships

Parenting is a tough job, and no one always gets it right. But one of the most important things you can do as a parent is to nurture a positive and secure relationship with your child. A strong parent-child relationship builds the foundation for a happy and fulfilling life for you and your child.

There are many ways to create and maintain a positive and nurturing environment for your child. This section will discuss tips and strategies for fostering a strong and loving parent-child relationship.

Be Open and Honest

Communication is vital to any successful relationship; the parent-child relationship is no exception. When you communicate with your child, listen actively and respond honestly. For example, encourage your child to express their feelings and concerns unreservedly and offer support and guidance when needed. Remember that communication is a two-way street. It would be best to share your thoughts and feelings with your child. Be open, honest, and transparent with your child. They will trust and respect you for it.

Spend Quality Time Together

Spend quality time with your child regularly. This does not have to be a big, elaborate event. Even 15 minutes of one-on-one time each day can make a big difference. During this time, focus on your child and make them feel special. Engage in activities your child enjoys and use this time to connect with them emotionally.

Show Affection and Gratitude

Showing affection and gratitude is another way to nurture a positive parent-child relationship. Express your love, appreciation, and gratitude to your child regularly. Hugs, kisses, and kind words can go a long way in making your child feel secure, loved, and valued.

Set Boundaries and Provide Guidance

As a parent, setting boundaries and advising your child is crucial. This creates a sense of safety and structure for your child and develops a strong sense of right and wrong in them. When setting boundaries, be clear, consistent, and fair. And when providing guidance, do so with love, respect, firmness, and a clear sense of authority.

Nurturing a positive and loving parent-child relationship requires effort and dedication, but the rewards are immeasurable. By communicating openly and honestly, spending quality time together, showing affection and gratitude, setting boundaries, providing guidance, and being a positive role model, you can help your child develop a solid and loving relationship with you that will last a lifetime. The next chapter will explore screen-free activities you can do as a family to foster strong family connections. The home, after all, is where love and support truly begin.

Chapter 2: Screen-Free Activities

With the rise of digital media, it has become increasingly difficult for families to spend quality time together without distractions from screens. When parents and their children are disconnected, a lack of meaningful interaction leads to misunderstandings and potential conflict. Regaining activities that foster face-to-face interaction is vital to improving communication and creating strong bonds within the family.

This chapter discusses the importance of screen-free time and making space for meaningful connections within the family. It outlines activities encouraging parent-child bonding through creative, interactive, and hands-on experiences. The activities featured in this chapter cater to different age groups and interests; everyone can find something they enjoy!

Benefits of Face-to-Face Interaction

Face-to-face interaction with your children can improve communication skills.
https://www.pexels.com/photo/child-hugging-a-woman-face-to-face-7173482/

Most families struggle to prioritize face-to-face interaction over screen time in today's digital age. However, screen time negatively impacts social-emotional development in children. Therefore, families must participate in screen-free activities to promote interpersonal communication and connection. This section explores the benefits of face-to-face interactions and some fun, screen-free activities that families can share.

- **Improved Communication Skills:** Face-to-face conversations allow nonverbal cues and body language to complement spoken words, which is essential for effective communication. By practicing personal interactions, children learn how to read social cues, develop empathy, and express themselves better, setting them up for success in personal and professional relationships.
- **Opportunity to Build Strong Relationships:** Personal interactions help you to develop a deep connection with your loved ones, creating a sense of belonging and unity. Family activities like board games, hiking, and making meals together offer an opportunity to bond over specific interests and shared experiences. These activities create memories that last a lifetime and strengthen familial relationships.
- **Better Mental Health:** According to the American Psychological Association, excessive screen time can lead to health issues, such as sleep deprivation, obesity, and poor academic performance. Conversely, face-to-face interactions affect mental health positively. For example, personal conversations have a calming effect on the brain, promoting positive feelings and reducing stress levels.
- **Improved Attention and Focus Skills:** People who spend less time on screens tend to have better mental focus and attention skills. Screen-free activities like playing sports, creating arts and crafts, or practicing mindfulness exercises facilitate mental de-stress, translating to better performance in school and other activities.

While avoiding technology altogether is impossible, prioritizing face-to-face interactions can bring your family closer, create lasting memories, and promote emotional well-being. Incorporating screen-free activities into your routine can help you strengthen relationships, have fun, and reap the positive benefits of personal interactions. So, it's time to put down the screens and start connecting.

Board Game Nights

Board games are one of the most enjoyable screen-free activities.
https://unsplash.com/photos/NrS53eUKgiE?utm_source=unsplash&utm_medium=referral&utm_content=creditShareLink

Playing board games with friends and family is a fun way to strengthen relationships while enjoying some competitive fun. This section explores some exciting board game night ideas that are screen-free and perfect for families to enjoy together.

Activity 1: Classic Board Games: Nostalgia and Learning in Every Move

Classic board games are a nostalgic way to bring generations together for a night of laughter and competition. These games offer entertainment and valuable learning experiences for players of all ages.

Step-by-Step Instructions:

1. Choose the Game: Select a classic board game like Monopoly, Scrabble, or Clue. Consider the preferences and ages of the players involved.
2. Set Up: Unfold the game board and distribute playing pieces, cards, and accessories. Review the rules together.
3. Take Turns: Begin the game by rolling dice or drawing cards to determine the order of play. Take turns clockwise, following the game's rules.
4. Follow the Rules: Read and follow the rules for each game. Make strategic decisions like buying properties, forming words, or solving mysteries.
5. Engage in Gameplay: Engage in the game, trading properties, forming words, or solving mysteries, depending on the game chosen.

6. Learn and Adapt: Embrace the learning aspect of the game. Monopoly teaches about money management, Scrabble enhances vocabulary, and Clue sharpens deductive reasoning.
7. Finish the Game: Continue playing until a predetermined goal is reached, such as bankruptcy in Monopoly or solving the mystery in Clue.
8. Celebrate the Winner: Congratulate the winner and reflect on the fun moments and strategic moves during the game.

Benefits:
- Multi-generational Bonding: Classic games bridge generation gaps, enabling grandparents, parents, and children to bond over shared experiences.
- Educational: Each game imparts unique skills. Monopoly teaches financial literacy, Scrabble enhances language skills, and Clue boosts critical thinking.

Activity 2: Cooperative Games: Teamwork and Triumph Unite

Cooperative board games foster a sense of unity as players collaborate to overcome challenges. These games teach invaluable teamwork and communication skills.

Step-by-Step Instructions:
1. Select the Game: Choose a cooperative game like Forbidden Island or Pandemic. These games require players to work together to achieve a common goal.
2. Understand the Objective: Familiarize everyone with the game's objective, whether recovering treasures or saving the world from a pandemic.
3. Assign Roles: Assign roles or characters to each player, each with unique abilities contributing to the team's success.
4. Discuss Strategy: Collaborate on a game plan. Share ideas, suggest moves, and consider the best course of action.
5. Take Turns: Follow the game's turn-based structure. Each player makes decisions to advance the team's progress.
6. Utilize Abilities: Make the most of each character's abilities to tackle challenges and obstacles.
7. Communicate Effectively: Constant communication is key. Discuss strategies, potential risks, and cooperative moves.
8. Work Towards Victory: Strive to achieve the game's objective as a team. Adapt and adjust strategies as new challenges arise.
9. Celebrate Victory: Celebrate a team victory with a sense of shared accomplishment, highlighting key contributions from each player.

Benefits:
- Team Bonding: Players develop a strong sense of unity and camaraderie as they work together towards victory.
- Communication Skills: Cooperative games enhance communication and decision-making skills as players must discuss strategies and coordinate actions.

Activity 3: Strategy Games: Unleashing Tactical Brilliance

Strategy board games provide intellectually stimulating experiences that demand critical thinking, planning, and astute decision-making.

Step-by-Step Instructions:

1. Choose the Game: Opt for a strategy game, such as Settlers of Catan, Ticket to Ride, or Risk. These games offer complex challenges.
2. Setup: Set up the game board, distribute resources or cards, and place playing pieces as per the game's instructions.
3. Understand Rules: Familiarize players with the chosen strategy game's rules, victory conditions, and gameplay mechanics.
4. Initial Moves: Make strategic opening moves that set the tone for your gameplay. Plan your early game actions carefully.
5. Strategic Decision-making: Analyze the evolving game state, make calculated decisions, and predict opponents' moves.
6. Resource Management: Manage resources, territories, or assets efficiently to gain advantages over opponents.
7. Long-term Planning: Develop a long-term strategy, focusing on victory conditions while adapting to the ever-changing landscape.
8. Interaction: Engage with opponents diplomatically or competitively to forge alliances or seize opportunities.
9. Tactical Maneuvers: Execute tactical maneuvers that outwit opponents and maximize your chances of victory.
10. Claim Victory: Achieve victory conditions specific to the game. Revel in the satisfaction of a well-executed strategy.

Benefits:

- Cognitive Stimulation: Strategy games exercise critical thinking, problem-solving, and strategic planning skills.
- Friendly Competition: Strategic challenges create an intellectually engaging and friendly competitive environment.

Activity 4: Party Games: Unleash Creativity and Laughter

Party board games inject a dose of creativity and lightheartedness into gatherings, sparking laughter and social interaction.

Step-by-Step Instructions:

1. Pick a Game: A party game like Telestrations or The Resistance is designed for larger groups and fosters interaction.
2. Explain the Rules: Explain the game's rules, emphasizing the creative or social aspects that players will engage with.

3. Create Teams: Divide players into teams or assign roles, depending on the game. Ensure everyone understands their roles.
4. Engage Creatively: Participate in creative challenges, drawing, acting, or deciphering clues based on the game's requirements.
5. Social Interaction: Interact with teammates and opponents through playful banter, creative interpretations, and collaboration.
6. Friendly Competition: Embrace the competitive spirit while maintaining a lighthearted atmosphere. Enjoy the humorous mishaps that unfold.
7. Celebrate Efforts: Celebrate creative efforts, amusing interpretations, and the fun moments that arise during the game.

Benefits:
- Creativity: Players tap into their creative wells, expressing ideas through drawings, acting, or wordplay.
- Stress Relief: Light-hearted gameplay acts as a stress reliever and energizer, fostering a positive mood.

Activity 5: DIY Board Games: Crafted Fun and Learning

Designing your own board game unleashes creativity and provides an opportunity to learn about game design, rules, and artistic expression.

Step-by-Step Instructions:
1. Brainstorm Ideas: As a family, brainstorm game concepts, themes, and mechanics. Let the imagination flow.
2. Design the Board: Create a game board using materials like cardboard, paper, or digital tools. Incorporate spaces, paths, or regions.
3. Craft Game Components: Design and craft game pieces, cards, dice, or any elements required for gameplay.
4. Define Rules: Collaboratively establish game rules, victory conditions, and mechanics that ensure balance and engaging gameplay.
5. Test and Refine: Playtest the game to identify flaws, imbalances, or areas needing improvement. Refine rules and mechanics accordingly.
6. Artistic Expression: Encourage artistic expression through designing visuals, illustrations, and thematic elements.
7. Play Your Creation: Enjoy playing the game you've created together. Celebrate the unique aspects and creativity of your homemade game.

Benefits:s
- Creative Outlet: DIY games nurture creativity by allowing players to shape their own rules, designs, and gameplay mechanics.
- Collaboration: Designing a game together fosters collaboration, communication, and compromise among family members.

Game nights are the perfect solution for screen-free family fun. Not only do they provide an opportunity for family bonding, but they also help children develop valuable skills like critical thinking, teamwork, and problem-solving. Whether you're playing classic games, cooperative games, strategy games, party games, or creating your own DIY board game, there is always something for everyone to enjoy.

Scavenger Hunts

In a world often dominated by screens, scavenger hunts present a refreshing opportunity for families to disconnect, bond, and embark on exciting adventures together. From classic hunts to themed explorations, this section is a treasure trove of scavenger hunt ideas that kindle the spirit of teamwork and ignite creativity, all while fostering beautiful memories.

Activity 6: Classic Scavenger Hunt: Traditional Thrills Await

Classic scavenger hunts offer timeless excitement as families work together to uncover hidden treasures within a set time frame.

Step-by-Step Instructions:
1. Create the List: Craft a list of items to be found. Tailor it to your location, whether indoors or outdoors. Make it diverse and engaging.
2. Set the Rules: Establish guidelines, such as collecting one item per person or assigning specific items to individuals.
3. Gather Supplies: Provide participants with bags, baskets, or containers to collect their findings.
4. Begin the Hunt: Announce the start and let the adventure unfold as family members seek out items on the list.
5. Collaborate: Encourage teamwork by assisting each other in finding items. Share strategies and discoveries.
6. Track Progress: As items are found, check them off the list. Keep track of time to maintain excitement.
7. Finish Line: Once the time is up, gather to compare findings and celebrate the collective efforts.

Benefits:
- Family Bonding: Classic hunts encourage communication, collaboration, and shared achievement.
- Observation Skills: Participants sharpen their observation skills while searching for items.

Activity 7: Themed Scavenger Hunt: Igniting Creativity Through Themes

Themed scavenger hunts infuse creativity and enthusiasm by centering the adventure around specific interests, from nature to photography.

Step-by-Step Instructions:
1. Choose the Theme: Select a theme aligned with your family's interests, such as nature, colors, or music.
2. Craft the List: Design a list of items or tasks related to the chosen theme. Incorporate a mix of easy and challenging elements.
3. Gather Tools: Equip participants with tools that enhance the experience, such as cameras for a photography-themed hunt.
4. Commence the Hunt: Reveal the theme and task participants with finding or capturing items that fit the theme.
5. Creative Interpretation: Encourage participants to interpret the theme creatively, sparking innovation and imagination.
6. Share Discoveries: Reconvene to share findings or creations. Discuss the thought process behind each discovery.
7. Acknowledge Creativity: Celebrate not just the items found but also the inventive ways the theme was embraced.

Benefits:
- Creative Expression: Themed hunts nurture creativity and imaginative thinking.
- Memorable Moments: The hunt's theme creates unique memories tied to a shared experience.

Activity 8: Puzzle Scavenger Hunt: Unraveling Challenges Together

Puzzle scavenger hunts merge brain-teasing challenges with the thrill of discovery, offering an intellectually stimulating adventure.

Step-by-Step Instructions:
1. Craft Puzzles: Devise puzzles and riddles that lead to the location of items. Include logic puzzles, anagrams, or codes.
2. Create Clues: Develop clues that progressively unveil the next puzzle or location, forming a trail of challenges.
3. Distribute Clues: Hand out the initial clue to start the hunt. Each solved puzzle leads to the next step.
4. Solve as a Team: Collaborate to solve puzzles, pooling diverse strengths and perspectives.
5. Navigate Challenges: Overcome the puzzle hurdles to reach the final location where a prize or item awaits.
6. Celebrate Achievements: Commend everyone's puzzle-solving prowess and relish the accomplishment together.

Benefits:
- Critical Thinking: Puzzle hunts stimulate analytical thinking and problem-solving skills.
- Collaborative Spirit: Participants collaborate to decode clues, enhancing teamwork.

Activity 9: Glow-in-the-Dark Scavenger Hunt: Illuminating Nighttime Adventure

Introduction: A glow-in-the-dark scavenger hunt adds a touch of enchantment to evenings, transforming the hunt into a magical escapade.

Step-by-Step Instructions:
1. Glowing Preparations: Set the stage using glow-in-the-dark paints, stickers, or items hidden under black lights.
2. Hide Items: Conceal glow-in-the-dark items throughout the designated area, creating an intriguing landscape.
3. Equip with Black Lights: Provide participants with black lights or UV flashlights to uncover the hidden treasures.
4. Explore the Darkness: Embark on the adventure, discovering glowing surprises along the way.
5. Create Clues: Incorporate clues or challenges that lead participants to the next glowing discovery.
6. Celebrate Discoveries: Revel in the magic of glowing finds and celebrate the shared adventure.

Benefits:
- Magical Experience: Glow-in-the-dark hunts infuse an element of wonder and magic into the adventure.
- Nighttime Bonding: Engaging in an activity after dark enhances family togetherness.

Activity 10: Around the House Scavenger Hunt: Indoor Delights

When the weather or circumstances keep you indoors, an around-the-house scavenger hunt promises indoor excitement and connection.

Step-by-Step Instructions:
1. Compile a List: Assemble a list of items found within the house. Ensure a mix of easy and challenging items.
2. Distribute the List: Hand out the list to participants, sparking anticipation for the indoor adventure.
3. Search and Seek: Engage in a lively search throughout the house, seeking items listed on the scavenger hunt.
4. Show and Share: Gather the items as they are found. Share interesting or amusing aspects of each discovery.
5. Creative Connections: Use the hunt to explore your living space in novel ways, connecting with familiar surroundings.
6. Celebrate the Hunt: Celebrate not just the items found but the laughter and interaction enjoyed along the way.

Benefits:
- Indoor Adventure: Around-the-house hunts offer indoor excitement and exploration.
- Observational Skills: Participants fine-tune their observation skills while engaging in an indoor quest.

Scavenger hunts are a great way for families to bond, engage more in screen-free activities, and have fun while being creative. The options are endless, and you can customize the hunt according to your family's interests and preferences. So, plan a scavenger hunt for your family and create fantastic memories.

Storytelling and Writing Sessions

Engaging in storytelling and writing sessions as a family is a heartwarming way to cultivate connections and kindle creativity. These activities offer a canvas for shared imagination and facilitate emotional and intellectual growth in children. In this section, you'll explore the magic of storytelling and writing sessions as remarkable screen-free family endeavors.

Storytelling sessions can help parents and children unleash their creativity.
https://www.pexels.com/photo/topless-man-covering-face-with-hands-7504929/

Activity 11: Storytelling Sessions: Crafting Tales from the Heart

Storytelling sessions are portals to enchanting worlds that can be woven anytime, anywhere, without the need for equipment or technology.

Step-by-Step Instructions:
1. Choose the Moment: Set the stage for storytelling during bedtime, meals, or family gatherings.

2. Take Turns: Invite each family member to take turns sharing stories about their day, cherished experiences, or beloved memories.
3. Build Upon Novels: Elevate the experience by extending the narratives of the novels you're reading. Introduce new characters, settings, or imaginative twists.
4. Embrace Creativity: Encourage inventive storytelling by embracing unexpected twists, vibrant characters, and imaginative scenarios.
5. Active Listening: Engage in active listening as each family member shares their tale, fostering appreciation for each other's creativity.

Benefits:
- Family Bonding: Storytelling sessions create bonds as family members share, listen, and engage in each other's narratives.
- Imagination Enhancement: The open-ended nature of storytelling nurtures creativity and imaginative thinking.

Activity 12: Writing Sessions: Penning Creativity and Imagination

Writing sessions allow family members to channel their creativity and explore the limitless expanse of imagination.

Step-by-Step Instructions:
1. Designate Writing Time: Set aside a dedicated time during the week for family writing sessions.
2. Generate Prompts: Provide prompts that spark creativity or use picture books as inspiration for your child's writing journey.
3. Encourage Exploration: Urge your child to explore a spectrum of topics, from fantastical tales to real-life adventures.
4. Shared Space: Write together in a shared space, fostering a sense of togetherness while pursuing individual creativity.
5. Celebrate Diversity: Celebrate the uniqueness of each family member's writing style and ideas, promoting self-expression.

Benefits:
- Creative Outlet: Writing sessions provide a creative outlet for imaginative expression.
- Language Skills: Participants enhance their language skills, vocabulary, and writing proficiency.
- Confidence Building: Sharing written work fosters confidence and a sense of accomplishment.

Activity 13: Storytelling with Props: Enchanting Narratives Unfold

Elevate storytelling sessions with a touch of whimsy by introducing props that infuse interactive magic into the narrative.

Step-by-Step Instructions:
1. Gather Props: Collect an array of props like soft toys, hats, or random objects that can be woven into stories.

2. Prop Selection: Allow your child to select a prop; this becomes a catalyst for their storytelling adventure.
3. Interactive Storytelling: As your child narrates their tale, encourage family members to embody the characters using the chosen props.
4. Immersive Experience: Immerse in the story as it unfolds with props, breathing life into characters and scenarios.
5. Rotating Roles: Let each family member choose a prop and take turns telling enchanting stories.

Benefits:
- Immersive Engagement: Props turn storytelling into an immersive experience, sparking creativity and participation.
- Family Interaction: The interactive element deepens family engagement and sparks laughter and shared delight.

Activity 14: Collaborative Storytelling: A Tapestry of Shared Imagination

Collaborative storytelling is a dynamic avenue to foster teamwork, creativity, and effective communication among family members.

Step-by-Step Instructions:
1. Initiate the Tale: Start the storytelling journey with a captivating opening, setting the stage for collaborative creation.
2. Passing the Baton: After a segment of the story, pass the storytelling "baton" to the next family member to continue the narrative.
3. Twists and Turns: Encourage creative contributions by adding surprising twists, unexpected characters, and imaginative settings.
4. Inclusive Participation: Ensure each family member has a chance to contribute, embracing diverse perspectives.
5. Dynamic Progression: As the story unfolds, witness the evolving tale shaped by each storyteller's input.
6. Conclusion: Bring the narrative to a satisfying close, celebrating the collective journey of imagination.

Benefits:
- Shared Creativity: Family members contribute unique elements, resulting in a tapestry of creativity.
- Joy of Creation: Witnessing the evolving story fosters a sense of shared accomplishment and delight.

Activity 15: Writing Competitions: A Literary Voyage of Fun

Infuse excitement into writing sessions by transforming them into friendly competitions, kindling enthusiasm and creativity.

Step-by-Step Instructions:

1. Set Competition Intervals: Designate regular intervals for writing competitions – weekly or monthly, based on preference.
2. Choose Themes or Prompts: Assign themes or prompts that challenge participants' creativity while inspiring their written work.
3. Writing Window: Allocate a specific time frame for participants to craft their stories based on the given theme.
4. Read Aloud: Have each participant read their stories aloud, sharing their imaginative creations with the family.
5. Voting and Recognition: Engage in voting to determine the winning story. Recognize and celebrate each participant's efforts.
6. Prizes and Rewards: Award the winner with a chosen prize – a favorite snack or a day of family fun.

Benefits:

- Friendly Competition: Writing competitions infuse fun and motivation into the creative process.
- Creative Challenge: Themes and prompts challenge participants to think outside the box and explore new horizons.

Storytelling and writing sessions can be a great way to engage your children's imaginations and develop their communication and creativity skills. These activities also help families spend quality time together and foster a love for storytelling and reading or even awaken a new talent. Furthermore, the lack of screens during these activities should lead to a more enjoyable and memorable experience for the whole family. So, set aside some time every week to explore your imagination through storytelling and writing sessions.

DIY Science Experiments

In an age dominated by screens, fostering creativity and exploration beyond technology becomes essential. One remarkable way to achieve this is by conducting captivating science experiments at home. These hands-on activities engage, educate, and bring families closer together. Here, we delve into captivating DIY science experiments that promise screen-free family excitement.

Activity 16: Make a Lava Lamp: Unveil the Magic of Chemistry

Crafting a lava lamp is a mesmerizing science experiment that promises wonder and amazement.

Step-by-Step Instructions:

1. Gather Materials: Collect a jar, water, oil, food coloring, and Alka-Seltzer tablets.

2. Water and Color: Fill a quarter of the jar with water and add a few drops of food coloring for a vibrant effect.
3. Oil and Jar Filling: Pour oil into the jar until it's three-quarters full, creating distinct layers.
4. Alka-Seltzer Magic: Break an Alka-Seltzer tablet into small pieces and drop them into the jar.
5. Observing the Transformation: Witness the captivating display as the tablet reacts with water, causing oil bubbles to rise, resembling a lava lamp.

Benefits:
- Scientific Phenomenon: Unveil the chemistry behind the mesmerizing motion.
- Visual Delight: Engage in captivating visual observation as the experiment unfolds.

Lava Lamp Mini Shaker

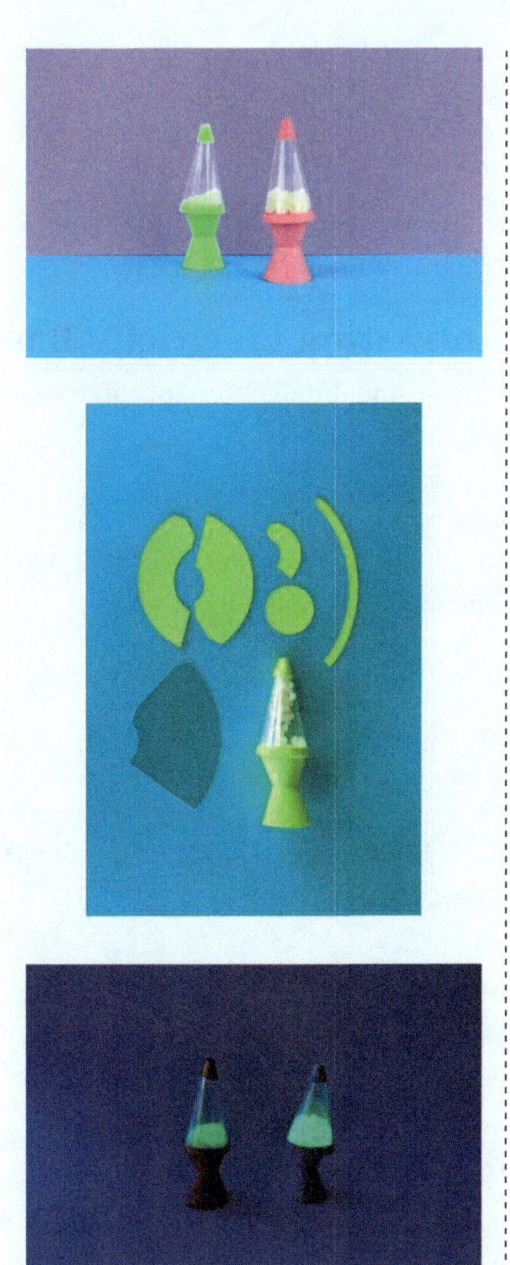
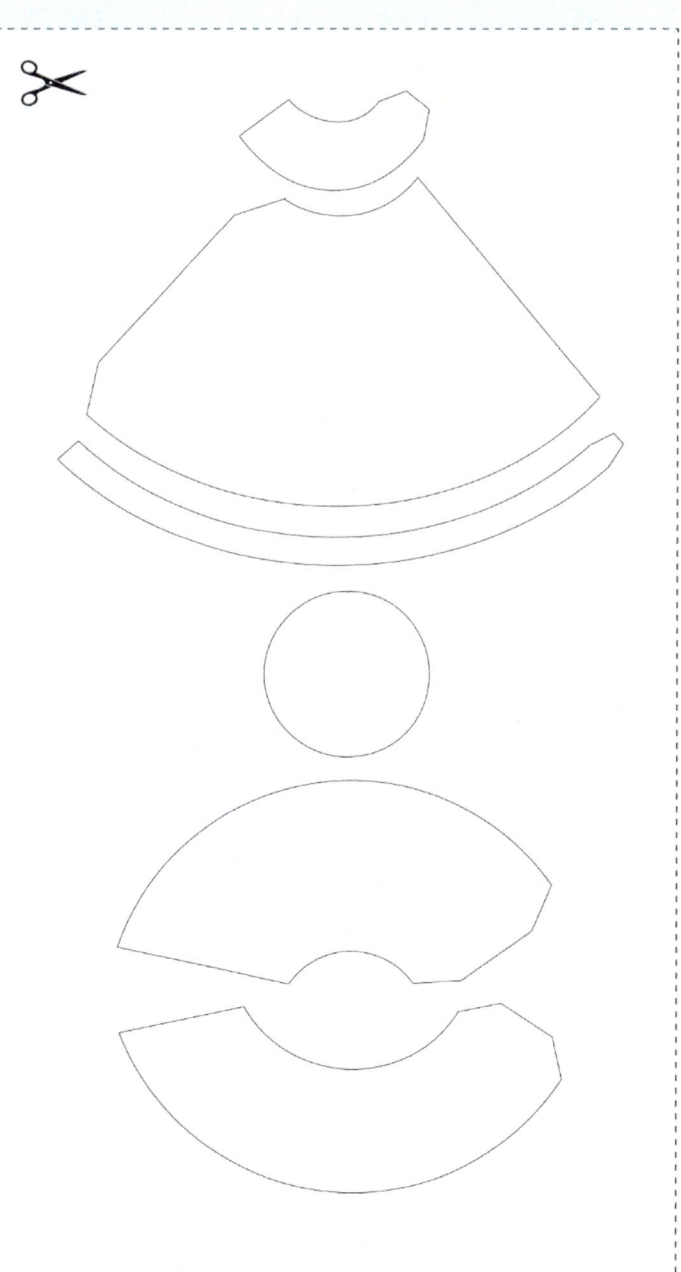

Activity 17: DIY Slime: A Sensory Exploration

Crafting your slime offers a tactile and imaginative journey into the world of science.

Step-by-Step Instructions:
1. Gather Ingredients: Collect PVA glue, borax powder or saline solution, and optional food coloring.
2. Mixing and Kneading: Combine the glue with Borax or saline solution until the mixture forms a cohesive ball.
3. Adding Color: Enhance the visual appeal by introducing food coloring and kneading until the color is evenly distributed.
4. Texture Exploration: Experience the tactile joy of stretching and manipulating the slime.

Benefits:
- Tactile Engagement: Creating and playing with slime provides a sensory-rich experience.
- Exploration of Properties: Participants explore the behavior of non-Newtonian fluids.

Activity 18: Create a Simple Circuit: Illuminating Electricity Basics

Introducing your children to the world of simple circuits lays the foundation for understanding electrical concepts.

Step-by-Step Instructions:
1. Assemble Materials: Prepare a battery, wire, and a lightbulb.
2. Wiring the Circuit: Connect the battery and lightbulb using the wire, forming a closed circuit.
3. Switch On: Activate the circuit by turning on the switch and observing the illumination of the lightbulb.

Benefits:
- Introduction to Electricity: Basic circuits offer a hands-on understanding of electrical flow.
- Visual Learning: Witnessing the lightbulb illuminate enhances comprehension.

Activity 19: Make a Crystal Snowflake: Winter Wonder in Science

Crafting crystal snowflakes blends winter wonder with science exploration.

Step-by-Step Instructions:
1. Gather Supplies: Collect Borax, pipe cleaners, boiling water, and a jar.
2. Pipe Cleaner Shapes: Bend pipe cleaners into snowflake designs, embracing creativity.
3. Borax Solution: Dissolve Borax in boiling water, creating a supersaturated solution.
4. Suspending Snowflakes: Suspend pipe cleaner snowflakes in the solution overnight.
5. Crystal Formation: Wake up to exquisite crystal-covered snowflakes in the morning.

Benefits:
- Crystal Growth Understanding: Witness the process of crystal formation firsthand.
- Art and Science Blend: Crafting snowflake shapes adds an artistic flair to the experiment.

Activity 20: Balloon Rocket Experiment: Propelling Physics Fun

The balloon rocket experiment introduces physics in a playful and captivating manner.

Step-by-Step Instructions:

1. Arrange the Setup: Prepare a long string, a straw, a balloon, and tape.
2. String Anchoring: Thread the string through the straw, securing it to two fixed objects across the room.
3. Balloon Attachment: Inflate the balloon and tape it to the straw.
4. Air-Powered Zoom: Release the balloon, allowing it to propel along the string due to escaping air.

Benefits:

- Physics Exploration: Experience Newton's third law of motion in action.
- Interactive Learning: Witness the experiment's outcome firsthand, promoting engagement.

The goal isn't to demonize technology entirely but to create pockets of real-world connection within your digital life. By swapping screens for DIY board games, hands-on science experiments, and collaborative storytelling sessions, you've opened doors to laughter, shared experiences, and deeper bonds. These screen-free activities are investments in family memories. They'll foster creativity, communication, and problem-solving skills that will resonate long after the games are stored and stories are finished.

Chapter 3: Outdoor Adventure Ideas

From hiking along scenic trails to camping under the stars, the great outdoors offers endless opportunities for fun and exploration. Get your heart pumping with a whitewater rafting trip, or test your skills on a thrilling zip line course. No matter what your family enjoys, outdoor adventure is the perfect way to disconnect from screens and connect meaningfully to nature and each other. So, gear up and prepare to embark on an unforgettable journey that will create memories to last a lifetime!

Inspired by the YouTube channel Fernweh Chronicles, this chapter invites you to embark on outdoor activities with your family. Nature is the perfect playground for families, allowing parents and children to create special memories and deepen relationships. Whether you're a fan of the outdoors or just starting, the 15 activities listed in this chapter will bring your family closer together while enjoying the wonders of nature.

Activity 21: Nature Walks

Taking a nature walk as a family will allow you to soak up the beauty of the natural world.
https://www.pexels.com/photo/family-walking-on-path-1682497/

Nature walks offer a fantastic opportunity for families to spend quality time together while soaking up all the beauty and goodness the natural world has to offer. One can never underestimate the benefits of fresh air, exercise, and sunshine on our physical and emotional well-being. These are precisely what families get when they hit the trails for a nature walk. Whether a short stroll around the neighborhood park or a longer hike up a mountain trail, there's always something to discover and appreciate in nature.

Step-by-Step Instructions:
1. Choose a Trail: Select a trail suited to your family's fitness level and interests. Opt for shorter paths for younger participants.
2. Dress Comfortably: Wear weather-appropriate attire and comfortable footwear to fully relish the experience.
3. Pack Essentials: Bring essentials like water, sunscreen, insect repellent, and a small first-aid kit.
4. Capture the Moment: Equip yourselves with a camera or smartphone to capture the beauty of nature.
5. Embrace Discovery: Encourage family members to explore, ask questions, and appreciate the natural surroundings.
6. Engage the Senses: Listen to bird songs, breathe in the fresh air, and feel the textures of leaves and rocks.
7. Mindful Moments: Pause along the way for mindfulness, allowing each family member to soak in the tranquility.

Benefits:
- Stress Relief: The serene environment aids in stress reduction and emotional well-being.
- Natural Learning: Nature is a dynamic classroom, fostering curiosity and learning.

As parents plan their excursions, the environment should always be on their minds. It's essential to respect and care for nature as we enjoy it so we can continue to experience its wonders for years to come. With preparation, safety in mind, and flexibility in plans, nature walks are a surefire way to create unforgettable memories as a family.

Activity 22: Geocaching

This thrilling adventure is a modern-day treasure hunt that has become a global phenomenon for good reason. Geocaching is a treasure hunt with a high-tech twist. Using GPS coordinates and clues, you can uncover hidden caches all around the globe. It's a great way to discover new places, get outdoors, and challenge yourself. Plus, it's perfect for all ages, from families with children to solo adventurers.

Step-by-Step Instructions:

Gather the Essentials: Equip yourselves with a GPS device or smartphone with a geocaching app, a notepad, a pen, and small trinkets for trading.

1. Select a Cache: Browse geocaching websites or apps to choose a cache – a hidden container waiting to be discovered.
2. Navigate to Coordinates: Input cache coordinates into your GPS device or app, guiding you to the hidden treasure.

3. Search and Discover: Follow the GPS guidance to reach the cache's vicinity. Utilize hints and descriptions to narrow your search.
4. Retrieve and Trade: Once found, open the cache, sign the logbook, and explore the contents. You can trade trinkets while respecting the cache's guidelines.
5. Log Your Find: Record your discovery on the geocaching app or website to share your experience with the geocaching community.

Benefits:
- Problem-Solving: The hunt challenges problem-solving skills as you decipher clues and navigate the terrain.
- Global Community: Engage with a diverse community of geocachers, forging connections beyond borders.

Geocaching offers the perfect opportunity to teach kids about the environment and encourage them to be mindful of the natural world. So, grab your GPS device, lace up your hiking boots, and hit the trails for a geocaching adventure your family will never forget.

Activity 23: Gardening Projects

Gardening can be a wholesome and fulfilling adventure for the whole family. It brings you closer to nature and provides an opportunity for exercise and fresh air. Imagine your family outside, tending your garden, watching it flourish and grow. The opportunities are endless, from planting a vegetable garden to creating a butterfly garden. You could even take it a step further: If you have the available space, build a mini-farm with chickens or other animals.

Gardening as a family can help you appreciate the environment.
https://unsplash.com/photos/L0mBZjo-oRw?utm_source=unsplash&utm_medium=referral&utm_content=creditShareLink

Step-by-Step Instructions:
1. Select a Garden Theme: Decide on the type of garden you want.
2. Plan the Layout: Design the garden layout with input from every family member. Allocate spaces for each chosen plant.
3. Prep the Soil: Clear the chosen area of debris and enrich the soil with compost, setting the stage for healthy plant growth.
4. Planting Day: Gather the family and plant seeds or young plants according to your plan. Involve children in planting and watering.
5. Care and Nourish: Assign garden care responsibilities, from watering to weeding. Teach your children the importance of regular care.
6. Celebrate Growth: As plants flourish, celebrate their growth milestones together. Discuss the significance of each plant in the ecosystem.
7. Personalized Spaces: Allow each family member a dedicated area for personal expression, encouraging creativity through plant choice and decorations.

Benefits:
- Nurturing Bonds: Gardening fosters teamwork and a sense of shared accomplishment within the family.
- Life Skills: Gardening imparts patience, responsibility, and the joy of reaping what you sow.

Gardening is a sustainable and earth-friendly activity that makes you appreciate the environment meaningfully. With proper preparation, safety measures, and adaptability, you can ensure a fun and very visible experience for everyone.

Activity 24: RV Through National Parks

If you're looking for an adventure completely immersing you in nature, look no further than an RV trip through national parks. The idea of hitting the open road with your family in tow and exploring the stunning landscapes surrounding us is enticing, to say the least. The fresh air, the beauty of the surroundings, and the sense of freedom an RV trip provides can be a powerful experience.

Step-by-Step Instructions:
1. Plan Your Route: Research and select national parks that align with your family's interests and preferences. Design an itinerary that encompasses the best of each park.
2. Choose an RV: Opt for an RV that suits your family's size and needs. Ensure it's well-equipped for a comfortable journey. (RVs can be rented if you can't afford to buy one.)
3. Pack Essentials: Pack essentials, such as clothing, camping gear, food, water, and a first-aid kit.
4. Hit the Road: Embark on your adventure, driving through breathtaking landscapes and stopping at designated national parks.
5. Explore Nature: Enjoy outdoor activities like hiking, wildlife spotting, and scenic viewpoints. Encourage children to learn about the ecosystems.
6. Camp Under the Stars: Camp in designated areas within the parks or in nearby campgrounds. Set up a campfire, share stories, and gaze at the stars.

7. Respect Nature: Abide by park rules and Leave No Trace principles. Teach your children the importance of preserving the natural environment.

Benefits:
- Connection to Nature: RV trips foster a profound connection to nature, enriching family bonds.
- Physical Wellness: Outdoor activities promote physical fitness and well-being.

From Yosemite to Glacier National Park and everywhere in between, an endless array of national parks is waiting to be explored. With proper planning, safety measures, and flexibility, you can venture on a journey your family will never forget.

Activity 25: Go Trekking

Trekking is an adventurous way to explore new places and a fantastic opportunity to bond with your family, breathe in the fresh air, and take in stunning scenery. There's nothing quite like conquering a challenging trail together, high-fiving at the top of a mountain, and taking in a breathtaking view as a reward.

Step-by-Step Instructions:
1. Select Your Trail: Research and choose a trail suitable for your family's fitness level and interests.
2. Dress the Part: Wear comfortable, moisture-wicking clothing and sturdy footwear that offers proper support.
3. Pack Thoughtfully: Load up with essential items, such as snacks, water, a basic first-aid kit, a map, and a compass.
4. Safety First: Research the chosen trail in advance. Inform a trusted friend or family member about your plans.
5. Start the Journey: Set out on your trek with a positive attitude and a spirit of adventure. Take regular breaks to rest and enjoy the scenery.
6. Capture Memories: Bring a camera or smartphone to capture the picturesque moments along the way.
7. Bond and Connect: Engage in conversations, share stories, and play games during breaks to strengthen family bonds and create lasting memories.

Benefits:
- Physical Challenge: Trekking offers a full-body workout, boosting cardiovascular health and stamina.
- Family Bonding: Shared experiences in nature deepen connections and foster meaningful conversations.

It's essential to prepare for your trekking adventure properly. Dress appropriately, pack plenty of snacks and water, and research the trail ahead of time for information on the difficulty level and any safety concerns. And most importantly, remember to be flexible and adapt to unexpected changes in the weather or terrain.

Activity 26: Pan for Gold

Imagine a family adventure that blends the thrill of outdoor exploration with the allure of striking it rich. Panning for gold is an engaging escapade that involves teamwork, physical effort, and the excitement of discovering hidden treasures. As you plunge your hands into the earth, sift through gravel, and witness the glint of gold, you'll create enduring memories and forge unbreakable bonds with your loved ones.

Step-by-Step Instructions:

1. Select Your Location: Research local areas where gold panning is allowed. Look for spots with historical significance or areas known for gold deposits.
2. Gather Supplies: Acquire basic gold panning equipment, including a pan, shovel, and a container for collecting your findings.
3. Find the Right Spot: Head to the riverbank or a stream known for gold potential. Look for areas with slower-moving water and gravel bars.
4. Dig and Fill: Using your shovel, gather gravel and soil from the riverbed. Fill your pan about half-full with this mixture.
5. Submerge and Swirl: Submerge the pan in water, allowing water to flow in and wash away the lighter materials.
6. Fanning Technique: Use the fanning technique to remove excess material, leaving behind heavier particles that could be gold.
7. Focus on the Bottom: Tilt the pan slightly forward and gently shake it side to side to encourage gold to settle at the bottom.
8. Inspect and Collect: Carefully inspect the bottom of the pan. If you spot glimmers of gold, use tweezers or a small vial to collect your findings.

Benefits:

- Physical Activity: The process of digging, washing, and sifting engages muscles and provides a fun form of exercise.
- Bonding and Memories: As you work together to uncover gold, you create shared memories and strengthen family bonds.

With each sift of the pan, you're not just searching for gold. You're sifting through time, unearthing stories of the past, and sharing the spirit of adventure that has captivated explorers for generations. So, grab your pan, head to the riverside, and embark on a journey that promises both glittering treasures and cherished connections.

Activity 27: Clean Up, Connect, and Give Back: Family Fun with a Purpose in the Outdoors

Sunshine, fresh air, and a chance to make a difference. What better ingredients could you ask for in a family outing? Ditch the screens and head outdoors for a rewarding experience that combines community spirit with the joy of spending time in nature. Volunteering for a local park clean-up, beach clean-up, or community garden is a fantastic way to instill environmental awareness in your children while fostering teamwork and a sense of accomplishment.

Step-by-Step Instructions:
1. **Pick Your Project:** Dive into the heart of nature with a beach clean-up, or spruce up your neighborhood park. Community gardens often welcome helping hands too. Research local organizations or check online calendars for upcoming events.
2. **Gather Your Heroes:** Assemble your family heroes. From enthusiastic toddlers to responsible teens, everyone can contribute. Explain the importance of environmental stewardship and get them excited about their roles.
3. **Gear Up for Action:** Dress comfortably and weather-appropriately. Sunscreen, hats, water bottles, and snacks are essential. Don't forget reusable gloves and sturdy bags for collecting trash.
4. **Bond as You Pick:** Divide tasks according to age and abilities. Little ones can collect small litter, while older kids can tackle larger items. Teamwork makes the clean dream work.
5. **Treasure Hunt Time:** Turn trash collecting into a game. Challenge yourselves to find the most unusual piece of litter or create categories for different finds. Make it fun and educational.
6. **Celebrate Your Impact:** After a job well done, take a moment to appreciate your contribution. Discuss the positive impact you've made on the environment and your community.

Benefits:
- **Bonding Time:** Working together on a shared goal strengthens family ties and creates lasting memories.
- **Nature Connection:** Immerse yourselves in the outdoors, appreciate fresh air and sunshine, and learn about the local environment.
- **Civic Responsibility:** Instill a sense of community spirit and empower your children to make a positive difference.
- **Fitness Fun:** Get some exercise while having fun! Bending, walking, and carrying bags contribute to an active and healthy family outing.

Trade in your usual routine for an adventure with purpose. Grab your family, head outdoors, and volunteer your time for a clean-up project. You'll be amazed at the sense of accomplishment, the connection to nature, and the joy of giving back to your community, all while creating unforgettable family memories. Every little bit counts, and together, you will make a big difference.

Activity 28: Seaplane Adventure

If you're looking for an exciting way to bond with your children, a seaplane adventure is what you need. Not only will you get to ride on a unique aircraft, but you'll also be treated to breathtaking views of the ocean and surrounding landscapes. This experience will be fun and has its own educational and developmental benefits.

Step-by-Step Instructions:
1. **Choose a Reputable Provider:** Research and select a reputable seaplane tour provider that adheres to safety protocols and offers captivating routes.
2. **Plan Ahead:** Reserve your adventure in advance, ensuring availability and smooth logistics for your family.

3. Safety Briefing: Before takeoff, listen carefully to the safety briefing provided by the pilot. Familiarize yourselves with emergency procedures.
4. Buckle Up: Once onboard, ensure everyone is securely buckled up, ready to embark on this thrilling journey.
5. Capture the Moments: Bring along a camera or smartphone to capture the mesmerizing aerial views and the excitement on your family's faces.
6. Curiosity Unleashed: Encourage your children to ask questions about the landscape below, the plane's mechanics, and everything that piques their curiosity.
7. Enjoy the Experience: As you ascend above the water, let the sense of awe wash over you. Take in the panoramic views and cherish this moment of shared wonder.

Benefits:
- Educational Exploration: A seaplane adventure fuels children's curiosity and encourages them to learn about aviation, geography, and the natural world.
- Confidence and Adventure: Experiencing flight fosters confidence and an adventurous spirit as children engage with the world from a new perspective.

With this thrilling activity, you'll soar high above the water, taking in breathtaking views and experiencing a head rush like no other. But the benefits of a seaplane excursion go far beyond just the physical thrill. It's also a chance to connect with your loved ones, bond over a shared sense of adventure, and create memories that will last a lifetime.

Activity 29: Row Boating

Close your eyes and imagine yourself gliding through calm waters, surrounded by the beauty of nature. The gentle sounds of birds and water create a soothing symphony as you embark on a row boating adventure with your children.

Step-by-Step Instructions:
1. Choose Your Location: Research and select a suitable water body for row boating—be it a serene lake, a meandering river, or a calm inlet.
2. Safety First: Prioritize safety by equipping everyone with life jackets and ensuring you're familiar with the water's conditions.
3. Basic Rowing Technique: Familiarize your family with the basics of rowing, including how to hold the oars and navigate the boat.
4. Share Responsibilities: Assign roles to each family member, whether it's rowing, steering, or simply enjoying the ride.
5. Capture the Experience: Bring a waterproof camera or smartphone to capture the picturesque moments and the smiles on your family's faces.
6. Engage with Nature: Take moments to pause and immerse yourselves in the natural world around you.
7. Mindful Connection: Use the gentle rhythm of rowing to engage in meaningful conversations and enjoy each other's presence.

Benefits:
- Physical Activity: Row boating provides a full-body workout, enhancing cardiovascular health and building physical strength.
- Teamwork and Communication: Coordinating rowing actions fosters teamwork and communication, strengthening familial bonds.

As your family embarks on a row boating adventure, you'll bask in the beauty of nature and build cherished memories that will last a lifetime. So, gather your crew, launch your boat, and navigate the waters of togetherness and exploration.

Activity 30: Wildlife Safari

Imagine getting into a sturdy jeep and embarking on a thrilling adventure through the great outdoors with your loved ones, surrounded by the sounds and sights of majestic creatures in their natural habitat. The excitement of spotting a lion basking in the sun or a herd of grazing elephants is matched only by the emotional and physical benefits of this incredible experience.

Step-by-Step Instructions:
1. Choose Your Safari: Research and select a reputable wildlife reserve or national park known for its rich biodiversity and responsible conservation practices.
2. Guided or Self-Drive: Decide whether to embark on a guided safari with a knowledgeable ranger or opt for a self-drive adventure.
3. Pack Essentials: Prepare by packing essentials, such as binoculars, cameras, hats, sunscreen, insect repellent, and water to stay comfortable and capture memories.
4. Respect Wildlife: Emphasize the importance of respecting the animals and their habitat. Keep a safe distance and avoid disturbing their natural behaviors.
5. Stay Patient: Patience is key in wildlife observation. Spend time quietly observing and waiting for the animals to appear naturally.
6. Learn and Appreciate: Encourage your family to ask questions, learn about the animals, and appreciate the intricate balance of nature.

Benefits:
- Educational Experience: Wildlife safaris offer a unique educational opportunity for your children to learn about different species and ecosystems.
- Nature Immersion: Immerse yourselves in the natural world, gaining a deeper understanding of the delicate balance of life in the wild.

A wildlife safari is an exhilarating escapade and a rare opportunity to recharge and reconnect with nature, giving you a much-needed break from the hustle and bustle of daily life.

Activity 31: Stargazing

Gazing up at the stars has been a source of inspiration and discovery since time immemorial. This activity is more than just a fun experience. It encourages your little ones to explore their curiosity and creativity. Through stargazing, children learn about our universe's vastness and the planets and understand astronomy better.

Materials Needed:
- Telescope or Binoculars: Enhance your stargazing with a telescope or binoculars to observe celestial bodies more closely.
- Star Maps or Apps: Use star maps or smartphone apps to identify constellations and planets visible in the night sky.
- Blankets and Pillows: Create a cozy space for your family to lie down and comfortably gaze at the stars.
- Warm Clothing: Dress warmly to ensure comfort during nighttime stargazing sessions.
- Flashlights: Red-filtered flashlights are ideal for preserving your night vision.

Step-by-Step Instructions:
1. Choose a Clear Night: Pick a night with minimal light pollution for optimal stargazing visibility.
2. Location Matters: Find a quiet, open area away from city lights, such as your backyard, a park, or a camping site.
3. Set Up Comfortably: Lay out blankets and pillows to make a comfortable space for everyone to lie down and gaze at the sky.
4. Learn the Basics: Before heading out, familiarize yourself with a few key constellations and planets visible that night.
5. Use Star Maps or Apps: Use star maps or stargazing apps to help identify celestial bodies and constellations as you spot them.
6. Engage Curiosity: Encourage questions and discussions about what you're seeing. Explore topics like planets, stars, galaxies, and the cosmos.

Benefits for Families:
- Quality Time: Stargazing brings families together in a serene setting, fostering bonding and meaningful conversations.
- Wonder and Awe: Observing the vastness of the universe evokes a sense of wonder and humility, igniting curiosity in children.

By taking your little ones out to look up at the night sky, you introduce them to a beautiful world beyond our planet and create precious memories with your kids. Stargazing is a fantastic experience and an excellent way to bond with your family.

Activity 32: Camping

Camping can encourage your children to explore.
https://unsplash.com/photos/8-jqqr-rpo0?utm_source=unsplash&utm_medium=referral&utm_content=creditShareLink

When was the last time you spent time with your family, away from the hustle and bustle of modern life? Exploring the outdoors is a beautiful way to connect and experience nature's beauty together. Put up a tent, gather around a campfire, and sing songs while roasting marshmallows. Camping is the perfect getaway for you and your children.

Materials Needed:
- Tents and Sleeping Bags: Ensure you have suitable tents and cozy sleeping bags for everyone.
- Campfire Supplies: Pack firewood, matches, and fire starters for safe and enjoyable campfires.
- Cooking Gear: Don't forget a portable stove, pots, pans, utensils, and other cooking essentials.
- Food and Snacks: Plan and pack meals, snacks, and ingredients for a variety of dishes.
- Water and Hydration: Carry ample water bottles and a water purification system if needed.
- Clothing and Footwear: Pack weather-appropriate clothing, including rain gear and comfortable footwear.

- Outdoor Equipment: Consider bringing hiking gear, binoculars, and nature identification guides.
- First-Aid Kit: Ensure you have a well-stocked first-aid kit for any emergencies.

Step-by-Step Instructions:
1. Choose a Camping Site: Research and choose a camping site that suits your family's preferences and level of outdoor experience.
2. Prepare Camping Gear: Gather and check all camping gear, ensuring everything is in good condition and properly functioning.
3. Pack Essential Supplies: Pack tents, sleeping bags, clothing, food, cooking equipment, and other essentials.
4. Set Up Camp: Upon arrival, set up your tents, arrange sleeping areas, and establish a comfortable campsite layout.
5. Campfire Creation: Build a safe and controlled campfire in designated fire rings or areas.
6. Cook Delicious Meals: Utilize your cooking gear to prepare meals, allowing your family to enjoy hearty and nutritious food.
7. Bond around the Campfire: As the sun sets, gather around the campfire for storytelling, singing, and roasting marshmallows.
8. Practice Leave No Trace: Respect the environment by leaving your campsite clean and minimizing your impact on nature.

Benefits:
- Skill Development: Camping encourages problem-solving, critical thinking, teamwork, and adaptability.
- Technology Detox: Camping allows for a break from screens and technology, enabling true face-to-face interactions.

Camping is a great way to spend quality time with your family. It allows you to bond and create lasting memories in the great outdoors. So put on your backpacks, pack your tents and some snacks, and start planning for an unforgettable camping adventure!

Activity 33: Air Balloon Ride

Imagine the excitement of taking to the skies with your family in an air balloon! The breathtaking views, the serenity and peace up in the clouds, and the feeling of floating on a breeze are truly magical experiences.

Step-by-Step Instructions:
1. Choose a Reputable Operator: Research and select a reputable air balloon ride operator known for safety and exceptional experiences.
2. Plan Ahead: Make reservations in advance and choose a time that suits your family's schedule and preferences.
3. Dress Comfortably: Wear weather-appropriate clothing and comfortable shoes for the journey.

4. Arrival and Preparation: Arrive at the designated location and listen attentively to the pilot's safety instructions.
5. Take Off: As the balloon inflates, experience the thrill of takeoff, feeling the gentle lift as the balloon ascends.
6. Breathtaking Views: As you rise above the landscape, marvel at the breathtaking panoramic views below.

Benefits:
- Memorable Experience: An air balloon ride creates lasting memories that you and your family will cherish for years to come.
- Unique Perspective: Seeing the world from above provides a unique and captivating perspective on familiar landscapes.

The experience of floating in an air balloon will provide your family with some beautiful memories, help children appreciate nature's beauty from a different perspective, and awaken their sense of adventure.

Activity 34: Snow Skiing

A fantastic skiing adventure can be just the thing to get the family together and enjoy a thrilling experience with each other. Snow skiing is a sport that encourages your children to stay physically active while having fun. It can also help them learn the importance of patience, practice, and safety. In addition to the physical benefits, skiing will help your kids learn about teamwork.

Materials Needed:
- Ski equipment (skis, poles, boots, helmets)
- Ski clothing (waterproof jacket, pants, gloves)
- Goggles to protect eyes from sun and snow glare

Step-by-Step Instructions:
1. Choose the Right Destination: Research and select a skiing destination suitable for your family's skiing abilities, whether beginner or experienced.
2. Rent or Buy Equipment: If you don't already have skiing gear, rent or buy skis, poles, boots, and helmets for each family member.
3. Dress for Success: Wear appropriate ski clothing to keep warm and dry on the slopes, including waterproof jackets, pants, gloves, and goggles.
4. Safety First: Attend a brief lesson on skiing basics, including how to put on and use your gear, skiing techniques, and safety measures.
5. Start on Gentle Slopes: Begin on beginner slopes to build confidence and get comfortable with the skiing motion.
6. Take Skiing Lessons: Enroll in skiing lessons for beginners or intermediate skiers to improve your skills and gain confidence.

Benefits:
- Physical Activity: Skiing is a fantastic way to stay active and engage in a full-body workout while having fun.

- Life Skills: Learning to ski teaches patience, perseverance, and the importance of practice in achieving goals.

With ski resorts, snow parks, and other activities like zip lining and sledding, you and your family can enjoy a great time together, learning something new while having fun. So, grab your ski gear and hit the slopes for an unforgettable skiing experience!

Activity 35: Barbecue

Picture a sun-kissed afternoon in your backyard, with the tantalizing aroma of grilled food wafting through the air and the joyous sounds of laughter as your family gathers for a delightful barbecue. This culinary adventure isn't just about indulging in delicious food. It's a chance to create lasting memories while sharing the joy of cooking and quality time with your loved ones.

Materials Needed:
- Grill (charcoal, gas, or electric)
- Grilling utensils (tongs, brushes)
- Ingredients for chosen dishes
- Seasonings and marinades
- Outdoor seating and decorations

Step-by-Step Instructions:
1. Plan the Menu: Decide on a menu that includes a variety of foods to grill, such as burgers, hot dogs, vegetables, and even skewers.
2. Preparation Time: Gather the necessary ingredients, seasonings, and marinades for your chosen dishes. Invite your kids to help with preparations.
3. Fire Up the Grill: Preheat the grill and ensure it's clean and ready for cooking. Make sure you have the appropriate tools, such as tongs and brushes.
4. Grill the Goodness: Carefully place your chosen items on the grill and cook them to perfection.
5. Involvement of Children: Encourage your children to help with the grilling process. Teach them about grill safety and the art of flipping burgers.
6. Set the Scene: Arrange a comfortable outdoor dining area with seating, decorations, and a cozy atmosphere for the family to enjoy.

Benefits:
- Culinary Skills: Involving your children in the preparation and cooking process fosters valuable culinary skills and a sense of accomplishment.
- Life Lessons: Cooking teaches patience, cooperation, and the value of teamwork while preparing a meal together.

Gathering around the grill isn't just about savoring scrumptious food. It's an opportunity for your family to connect, engage in meaningful conversations, and enjoy each other's company in a relaxed and enjoyable atmosphere. As you share laughs, stories, and bites of mouthwatering food, your family barbecue will become a cherished tradition that brings everyone closer together. So, light up the grill, let the flavors dance, and celebrate the joy of cooking and togetherness in your backyard haven.

Whether you're in the mood for a scenic hike, a thrilling rafting trip, or a relaxing day at the beach, there's no shortage of possibilities when it comes to outdoor fun. This chapter provides some beautiful ideas on how to spend quality time with your family and create lasting memories together. From geocaching, nature walks, camping, air balloon rides, skiing, and barbecues, these adventures offer the perfect opportunity for bonding and creating lasting memories with your loved ones. So, it's time to grab the family and start exploring!

Chapter 4: Creative Souls: Unleash Your Inner Artists

There's an artist inside all of us waiting to be unleashed, and what better way to bring it out than with family? Creative souls can find inspiration in the most unexpected places, and sharing the process with loved ones makes it all the more rewarding. Whether painting, writing, pottery, or any other art form, making art together can deepen connections and build lasting memories. So, gather your family, grab some supplies, and let your inner artists run wild.

Activity 36: Creative Collages

Collages can be personalized to suit your family's style and interests.

https://unsplash.com/photos/LYDQWASezog?utm_source=unsplash&utm_medium=referral&utm_content=creditShareLink

From beginners to experienced artists, collages are the perfect creative outlet for anyone. Spend quality time with the family as you cut, paste, and create beautiful art together. Be it photographs or magazine clippings, the possibilities for collage materials are endless. In addition, collages can be personalized to represent your family's unique style and interests. With this activity, you'll tap into your creativity, bond with your loved ones, and create beautiful memories. Here's all you need to get started:

Materials Needed
- Scissors
- Glue or tape
- A variety of magazines, newspapers, cardboard, and other materials
- A board or canvas for the collage

Step-by-Step Instructions
1. Gather your supplies and decide on a theme for your collage.
2. Arrange the materials in an aesthetically pleasing pattern.
3. Cut and glue the pieces to your board or canvas.
4. Let your artwork dry before displaying it proudly!

Additional Ideas
- Create a family tree collage with pictures of your relatives
- Cut up old magazines and newspaper articles to create an abstract work of art
- Have each family member make their own unique collage. This can be a great display piece when hung side by side!
- Explore the world of mixed media and incorporate 3D elements like buttons, fabric, found objects, etc., into your collage.

Remember to have fun and enjoy the creative process regardless of your project type. Then, celebrate your masterpiece with a family photo or an online post. Sharing your artwork is a great way to show off the beautiful bond you have created together.

Activity 37: Family Murals

Creating art together as a family is a great way to foster a more profound sense of connection and creativity within your household. With family murals in particular, you can unleash your inner artist and collaborate to create something extraordinary. Whether creating a work of art to adorn the walls of your home or simply using it as an opportunity to bond, family murals are a fun and rewarding experience that everyone can enjoy. Don't worry if you're not the most artistically inclined person. The beauty of working on a mural is that everyone can contribute.

Materials Needed
- A large canvas or wall
- Acrylic paint in various colors
- Paintbrushes of different sizes
- Other materials (fabric, paper, beads), if desired
- Protective sheeting to cover the floor or wall

Step-by-Step Instructions

1. Start by cleaning the wall or canvas and laying down protective sheeting to cover the floor or wall.
2. Have each family member devise a design for their mural section and sketch it out.
3. Begin painting the mural one section at a time.
4. Once all the sections are complete, admire your masterpiece!

Additional Ideas

- Include meaningful symbols, quotes, or images that represent the family
- Make each mural section unique by including fabric, paper, beads, and more
- Have each family member sign their section with a message of love or encouragement
- Remember to document your creative process with photos or videos!

Working together on a family mural is an enriching way to express yourselves as individuals while uniting as a unit. The perfect combination of art and connection will leave a lasting impression on everyone. So, grab a paintbrush and let the creative juices flow.

Activity 38: Group Weaving Projects

Group weaving projects are an opportunity to get together with your loved ones and make something beautiful. Whether you are a seasoned weaver or a beginner, there are endless possibilities to explore. This section will provide all the information you need to create a wonderful weaving project with your loved ones.

Materials Needed

- Weaving loom or frame
- Yarn, thread, or wool
- Recycled materials or fabric scraps
- Scissors
- Tapestry needle
- Comb or fork
- Optional embellishments like beads, buttons, and feathers.

Step-by-Step Instructions

1. Set up your loom or frame by following the instructions on your purchased loom or by researching a tutorial on how to make your own.
2. Tie a ribbon, piece of yarn, or string to the top of the loom or frame to create a starting point.
3. Begin your weaving project by wrapping the yarn or wool around the loom or frame in a horizontal direction. Make sure to pull the thread tightly to avoid gaps.
4. After the first row is complete, push the yarn down with a fork or a comb to keep the row compact.
5. Start the second row by taking a piece of yarn or wool and weaving it under and over the first row of threads. Repeat this process and continue pushing down the rows as needed.

6. To change colors or add texture, tie or weave the next color into the end of the yarn or wool and continue weaving.
7. Once you have reached the desired length, tie off the end of the yarn and cut any excess.
8. Carefully remove the weaving project from your loom or frame, then tie the loose ends together or sew a border piece around the project.

Additional Ideas
- Consider making a collaborative weaving project where everyone contributes by adding their weaves.
- Make a themed weaving, such as a holiday decoration or a piece of art for a specific room in your home.
- Use different materials like ribbon, tulle, or lace to add texture and dimension to your weaving project.

Regardless of your skill level, you can enjoy the process of weaving and exploring different textures and colors. So, grab your loom or frame and various materials, and enjoy some quality time with your family or friends while unleashing your inner artist.

Activity 39: Family Talent Show

Call all aspiring singers, dancers, comedians, and magicians. Dust off your imaginary mics, grab your DIY props and get ready to dazzle the world (or at least your immediate family) with the ultimate family talent show. This activity is the perfect recipe for a night of laughter, memories, and unleashing hidden talents you never knew existed. What are you waiting for? It's time to turn your living room into a miniature Vegas stage.

Step-by-Step Instructions:
1. **Spread the Word:** Announce the upcoming extravaganza. Get everyone excited about showcasing their hidden (or not-so-hidden) talents. Let imaginations run wild with ideas for songs, dances, skits, magic tricks, or even puppet shows.
2. **Brainstorm:** Gather the family and have a brainstorming session. Encourage participation from even the shyest members. There's a talent for everyone. Make it a collaborative effort, allowing everyone to contribute ideas and costumes.
3. **Practice Makes Perfect (Optional):** While spontaneity is always welcome, a little practice will boost confidence and ensure smooth performances. Set aside some time for rehearsals, offering support and encouragement. It's all about having fun, not achieving perfection.
4. **Stage Set-Up:** Transform your living room into a vibrant performance space. Drape some sheets as curtains, gather pillows for an audience "seating area," and dim the lights for a dramatic effect. Get creative with decorations and props.
5. **Showtime:** Let the performances begin. Designate a family member as the MC, introducing each act with flair and encouraging the audience to cheer loudly. Here, enthusiasm is crucial.
6. **Award Silly Prizes:** After each act, shower the performers with silly prizes. The funnier, the better. Award categories like "Most Creative," "Most Enthusiastic," or "Most Likely to Go Viral." Let laughter and silly awards be the highlight, not competition.

7. **Celebration Time:** Once all the acts are complete, celebrate the amazing talent (and courage) displayed. Take photos, capture videos, and reminisce about the funniest moments. Make it a night to remember.

Benefits:

- **Boosts Confidence:** Stepping outside your comfort zone and performing in front of loved ones will do wonders for self-confidence. It teaches kids (and adults) to embrace their individuality and celebrate their unique talents.
- **Strengthens Family Bond:** Working together towards a common goal, sharing laughter, and cheering each other on fosters a strong family connection and creates lasting memories.
- **Sparks Creativity and Expression:** This activity encourages imagination, creativity, and the freedom to express oneself uniquely. It's a fun outlet for everyone to tap into their inner artist and performers.
- **Unforgettable Fun:** This activity guarantees to bring laughter, silly moments, and heartwarming memories that will be cherished for years.

Ditch the screens, gather your family, and unleash your inner superstars. The goal is to have fun, be creative, and celebrate each other's unique talents (or lack thereof). Get ready for a night filled with laughter, applause, and unforgettable family moments. The curtain is about to rise on your very own Family Talent Show.

Activity 40: Painting Projects

Spending time as a family can be a heartwarming experience, but sometimes, it's hard to find the perfect activity to bring everyone together. Painting projects could be ideal if you want a fun and creative way to bond with your family. Whether you are an experienced artist or a beginner, painting can be a relaxing and entertaining activity for everyone in your family. This section will explore some painting project ideas you can do with your family and unleash your inner artist.

Painting can be a relaxing activity for all family members.
https://unsplash.com/photos/krV5aS4jDjA?utm_source=unsplash&utm_medium=referral&utm_content=creditShareLink

Materials Needed

Before starting on any painting projects, you will need to gather a few items:

- Paint brushes that are appropriate for the size of the canvas you plan to use
- A canvas or a sturdy board to paint on
- A palette to mix your colors
- Paint. Acrylic paints can be a great choice due to their quick-drying properties
- A jar of fresh water for cleaning brushes

Step-by-Step Instructions

Here are some simple steps to follow when starting a painting project with your family:

1. Choose a subject, such as a landscape or a portrait. You can also use stencils or tracing paper to create outlines before painting.
2. Lay down some old newspapers to protect your surroundings.
3. Mix the paints on your palette and prime your brushes with water to clean them.
4. Finally, start painting and experiment with colors and textures. You can even try some three-dimensional elements like glitter or sand.

Additional Ideas

There are many ways to make painting projects enjoyable and inspiring for your family. For example, you could try the following:

- Collaborating on a single painting
- Painting on unconventional surfaces like rocks, shoes, or recycled materials
- Creating a mural that each family member contributes to
- Hosting a painting contest that awards prizes for creativity or originality

Painting projects are a fantastic way to ignite your family's creativity, bring everyone closer together, and produce a beautiful piece of art. With these simple steps and some basic materials, you can have a fun-filled afternoon while creating a masterpiece you can all be proud of. It doesn't matter if you are a seasoned artist or a beginner; painting projects are a great way to express yourself and explore new ideas. But remember, the most important thing is to have fun and enjoy the experience together as a family!

Activity 41: Recycled Fashion Show

Are you tired of the usual family game nights? Craving an activity that sparks the imagination, embraces sustainability, and results in side-splitting laughter? Look no further than a Recycled Fashion Show. This unique event combines fashion design, eco-awareness, and friendly competition, creating memories that will last long after the final strut down the runway. **Materials Needed:**

- Recycled materials: newspapers, plastic bags, cardboard, fabric scraps, aluminum foil, anything goes.
- Scissors, tape, glue, and staplers
- Paints, markers, and other decorating supplies (optional)
- Empty boxes, chairs, or blankets to create a makeshift runway (optional)

- Silly props and accessories (optional)
- Prizes for "Most Creative," "Most Outrageous," and "Most Funniest" designs (optional)

Step-by-Step Instructions:

1. **Theme Time:** Decide on a fun theme for your fashion show, like "Ocean Odyssey," "Galactic Glam," or "Superhero Showdown." It will inspire your designs and add a layer of excitement.
2. **Design and Build:** Let imaginations run wild. Transform newspapers into flowing gowns, plastic bags into shimmering scales, and cardboard into sturdy armor. Encourage everyone to use their unique talents and styles.
3. **Accessorize and Embellish:** Add finishing touches with paint, markers, sequins, buttons, or anything else that catches your fancy. Don't forget the power of silly props and accessories to elevate your outfit.
4. **Runway Ready:** Create a makeshift runway using chairs, blankets, or even an empty hallway. Get ready for the spotlight with catchy music and enthusiastic announcers (family members, of course).
5. **Strike a Pose:** Show off your creations with confidence and flair. Strut your stuff, twirl, and pose for the "family judges" (who get to award those fun prizes, remember?).
6. **Celebrate Sustainability:** After the final catwalk, take a moment to appreciate the amazing designs created entirely from recycled materials. Discuss the importance of sustainability and how even small actions make a difference.

Benefits:

- **Boosts Creativity and Imagination:** Encourages families to think outside the box and utilize everyday materials uniquely.
- **Promotes Sustainability:** Raises awareness about the importance of recycling and reusing materials, fostering eco-conscious habits.
- **Builds Teamwork and Communication:** Requires families to collaborate on designs and support each other during the creation process.
- **Sparks Laughter and Fun:** Provides a lighthearted and engaging activity that will have everyone giggling and creating silly memories.
- **Strengthens Family Bond:** Creates a shared experience that fosters connection and understanding between family members.

Forget expensive costumes and fast fashion. A Recycled Fashion Show is all about embracing creativity, having fun, and celebrating sustainability with the people you love. Gather your recyclables, unleash your inner fashionistas, and get ready for a catwalk extravaganza that's sure to be anything but ordinary. The most important accessory is a big smile and a heart full of imagination.

Activity 42: Movie-Making Marathon

Have you ever wished to step onto the silver screen and create a cinematic masterpiece? Well, dust off your director's hat, gather your family crew and get ready for a thrilling adventure in filmmaking. A family movie-making marathon is the perfect way to unleash creativity, bond over a shared project, and end up with hilarious (and potentially award-winning) results. Grab your popcorn, dim the lights, and start rolling.

Materials Needed:
- Smartphones, tablets, or a basic video camera
- Tripod (optional, but highly recommended)
- Costumes, props, and set decorations (get creative with household items)
- Writing materials for your script
- Editing software (simple, free options are available online)
- Enthusiasm and a sprinkle of imagination

Step-by-Step Instructions:
1. **Theme Time:** Gather your family and brainstorm. Choose a fun genre to inspire your movie, like comedy, sci-fi, mystery, or even a superhero adventure. The possibilities are endless.
2. **Script and Storyboard:** It's time to become screenwriters. Collaborate on a short script, even if it's just a few pages. Create a storyboard to visually plan your scenes.
3. **Lights, Camera, Action:** Grab your camera and start filming. Assign roles within your family (actors, directors, camerapersons, sound technicians) and get creative with filming angles and shots. Don't worry about perfection, embrace the bloopers and have fun.
4. **Editing Magic:** Once you've filmed your scenes, it's time to edit. Use simple editing software to put your movie together, add music and sound effects, and create your masterpiece.
5. **Premiere Night:** Roll out the red carpet (or a blanket on the living room floor) and host a premiere night for your family and friends. Showcase your creation, enjoy some popcorn, and bask in the applause (and laughter).

Benefits:
- **Boosts Creativity and Imagination:** Encourages everyone to think outside the box and work together to bring a story to life.
- **Strengthens Family Bond:** Creates a shared experience that fosters communication, collaboration, and problem-solving skills.
- **Develops Technical Skills:** Introduces families to basic filmmaking techniques and editing software in a fun and engaging way.

A family movie-making marathon is more than just creating a film. It's about creating memories, laughter, and a sense of accomplishment together. Grab your cameras, unleash your inner Spielbergs, and get ready to yell "Action!" Who knows, your next blockbuster might just come from your living room.

Activity 43: Photography Challenges

With a camera and a few prompts, you can awaken your inner photographer and capture some fantastic memories. Suppose you're still trying to figure out where to start. In that case, we've got you covered with step-by-step instructions and additional ideas to inspire your creativity.

Materials Needed
- A camera (phone camera, point-and-shoot, or DSLR)
- A timer (optional)

- A list of prompts (see below for ideas)

Step-by-Step Instructions
1. Choose a prompt from the list below.
2. Set up your camera and timer (if using).
3. Take turns capturing photos that fit the prompt. You can interpret the prompt as creatively as you like.
4. Review your photos and choose your favorites.
5. Share your photos and discuss what you like about them.

Prompts:
- Self-portrait
- Something that makes you happy
- A shadow
- A pattern
- Something blue
- A close-up of nature
- A silhouette
- Something that represents family

Additional Ideas
- Turn your photo challenge into a scavenger hunt by hiding objects that fit the prompts and having family members find and photograph them.
- Make a time-lapse video by taking a photo every few seconds for a set amount of time.
- Print out your favorite photos and create a family photo album or wall display.

Photography challenges are a fun and creative way to spend time with family while capturing memories. With just a camera and some prompts, you can snap some fantastic photos you'll cherish for years.

From collages to murals, weaving to sculpture-making, there are endless possibilities for artistic exploration. So, let your imagination run wild as you pick up paintbrushes, cameras, and other tools to bring your ideas to life. And remember the thrill of a family art scavenger hunt, where you can uncover hidden gems and use them as inspiration for your next project. With these activities, you'll create beautiful pieces and strengthen bonds with your children.

Chapter 5: Revamping Game Night

If you're tired of the same old game night routine with your family, it's time to revamp it and bring some excitement back. With an open mind and a little creativity, you can turn your mundane game nights into memorable experiences that your loved ones will treasure. The key is offering various games, inventive variations on classic games, and new activities to keep everyone engaged.

This chapter will help you think outside the box and mix the types of games you usually play. It'll take you beyond the classic board games and introduce you to unique and unfamiliar games that are still fun for children and adults. You'll also find tips on creating a welcoming environment, fostering healthy competition, and promoting sportsmanship. The goal is to make game nights something your family looks forward to and cherishes.

Inventive Variations on Classic Games

Game nights with family can become monotonous and boring if you always stick to the same old games. Here are some inventive variations on classic games to add to the mix and take your family game night to the next level. From themed elements to DIY games, these new twists excite and spark your game night. So, grab your family and favorite board games, and let's play.

Revamping classic board games can make them more interesting for all family members.
https://unsplash.com/photos/0n7_eiAQZwA?utm_source=unsplash&utm_medium=referral&utm_content=creditShareLink

Activity 44: One-Word Story

Start with a single word, like "door." Each person adds one word, building a story sentence by sentence. You might end up with a thrilling adventure, a heartwarming tale, or a nonsensical yet hilarious journey. This simple game fosters creativity, listening skills, and unexpected twists.

Example:
- Player 1: Door
- Player 2: Creaks
- Player 3: Open
- Player 4: Revealing...

See where the story takes you!

Activity 45: Storytelling Dice Game

Create your own dice with prompts like characters (pirate, detective, astronaut), settings (castle, jungle, spaceship), and actions (runs away, solves a riddle, falls in love). Players roll the dice and create a collaborative story based on the results. This game is perfect for fostering imagination, improvisation, and teamwork.

Example:
- Player 1 rolls: Detective, Jungle, Climbs a Tree
- Player 2: "Our detective, lost in the dense jungle, must climb a towering tree to escape a pack of hungry monkeys."
- Player 3: "But as he reaches the top, he spots a hidden temple ruins..."

What adventures await next?

Activity 46: Blind Taste Test

Blindfold participants and have them taste different foods or drinks. Can they guess the ingredients and origin? This game is a fun way to explore new flavors, challenge preconceptions, and appreciate the complexity of taste.

Example:
- Food/Drink: Dark chocolate with chili flakes
- Player 1: "Hmm, I taste something sweet and spicy... maybe cinnamon and peppers?"
- Player 2: "I get a hint of bitterness too... could it be coffee with chili flakes?"
- Player 3: "Maybe dark chocolate with something savory... like bacon?"

Who has the most discerning palate?

Activity 47: Bringing Playwrights to the Party

Another creative way to revive your usual game night is to elevate it with some improvisational plays. Take turns being the host and set up scenarios on a game board. You can create storylines and character roles around the board. So, for example, in the game Scrabble, players can invent and act out a scene from a play using the words they've spelled.

Activity 48: Switching It Up

Finally, one of the simplest ways to refresh game night is to switch up the games and select a new game every week. Consider taking family polls to help come up with ideas. Depending on preference or play style, you can even have each family member play a different game. The idea is to keep the momentum going and maintain an element of surprise.

Family game nights are a time-honored tradition, but there's no reason it has to be boring. When you add a touch of imagination and creativity, you can reinvent classic games to make them fun and exciting. By mixing in themed elements, creating unique DIY games, hosting a family tournament, or even improvising some playwrights, you can ensure that game night will be a delightful and memorable evening for everyone.

Unique and Unfamiliar Games

It's game night with the family. Let's face it: we all want something new and exciting. With a library full of board and card games at home, it's easy to slip into a routine of always playing the same handful of games with loved ones. However, it's time to shake things up and overhaul game night with some unique and unfamiliar games. This section explores different categories of games that are just as fun but less familiar to you and your family. So, whether you're looking for a cozy night at home or a thrill-filled evening with your family, try out these exciting, non-digital games that will bring everyone closer together.

Activity 49: Artistic Games

Are you looking for a creative outlet for your family game night? Try out Pictionary, in which you must guess drawings made by others. Or unravel twisted tales with Dixit, where players create their stories and blend their imaginations to think of the right card.

Activity 50: Verbal Games

Oral games are perfect if you enjoy more personal games. These games challenge you to share secrets and push you out of your comfort zone, making them delightful and engaging. For example, in "Never Have I Ever," each player takes a turn stating something they have never done before, and if another player has done it, they take a sip of water or any beverage of their choice.

Activity 51: Musical Charades

Ditch the charades charades and express yourself through music. Hum, sing, or dance out movie titles, books, or even emotions. Challenge yourselves with different genres or instruments for added difficulty. This game is perfect for music lovers, party nights, and unleashing hidden talents.

Example:
- Theme: Sci-Fi Movie
- Player 1: Sings the iconic theme song from Star Wars
- Player 2: Dances a robotic jig representing Terminator

- Player 3: Humms the suspenseful theme from Alien

Can you guess the movie?

Activity 52: Roleplaying Games

Roleplaying games are the perfect fit for an innovative and interactive experience. Fans of Harry Potter can try their hands on Hogwarts Battle, while Game of Thrones followers could indulge in A Game of Thrones: The Board Game. These games are challenging and require multiple players to engage and work together.

Activity 53: Escape Room Games

The exit from the scary room with time ticking down adds a rush to the game, making it one of the most thrilling cooperative games out there. Escape rooms typically involve puzzles and riddles that players must figure out how to "escape" within the given time. Some ideas include The Heist and Escape from Atlantis.

Activity 54: Trivia Games

Trivia games make for a fun-filled and competitive night with your family. You can pick topics like history, music, sports, or pop culture and test each other's knowledge with games like Trivial Pursuit or Smart Ass. If you're looking for a unique twist, consider Quizizz or Kahoot!, which are games played on mobile devices.

Activity 55: Blindfolded Pictionary

One person draws a picture blindfolded while their partner describes it. The result? Hilarious misinterpretations and creative problem-solving. This game is perfect for large groups, laughter, and testing your communication skills.

Example:
- Player 1 (drawing): Scribbles furiously while blindfolded
- Player 2 (describing): "Okay, I see a circle... with, uh, something long coming out of it... and maybe a squiggle on top?"
- Player 1: Draws more lines and dots
- Player 2: "Hmmm... could it be a giraffe wearing a hat?"

Will they guess the right answer?

Your family game night doesn't have to be dull and monotonous, with the same tired board games or card games day after day. Instead, try out different game genres with your loved ones to create unforgettable memories. Whether trivia games, escape room games, or classic board games, the possibilities are endless, and the experiences can be upbeat and great fun. So, the next time you plan a family game night, pick an unfamiliar game and have fun trying it out with your loved ones.

Creating a Fun Atmosphere

Do you remember those game nights from your childhood? Chances are, you have fond memories of spending quality time with friends and family. However, with the advancement of technology, we spend less time connecting with loved ones in person. That is why revamping game night with family is a great way to bring everyone together and create lasting memories. But how do you make the experience more enjoyable?

Establishing Ground Rules

Everyone must know the rules before starting a game. Establishing the rules before the game begins prevents confusion and avoids disputes. Ensure that everyone understands the game's objective, how to score, and any other important rules.

Encouraging Good Sportsmanship

Good sportsmanship is essential for a fun family game night. Encourage your family to be gracious winners and good losers. Remind everyone that the objective is to have fun and spend quality time with one another, not compete. However, no one likes a sore loser, so everyone must practice respect, even amid defeat.

Keeping Score

It's important to keep score during game night, but it's equally important to maintain a healthy perspective on the score. Remember that the game score is not a reflection of personal abilities or worth but rather a measure of how well everyone played, which includes a bit of chance.

Creating an Engaging Environment

Creating a festive ambiance during game night will help everyone feel more relaxed and in good spirits. Decorate the game area with festive tablecloths and balloons. Light candles and play some feel-good tunes in the background. Another way to enhance the game atmosphere is by creating a special game night snack or potluck.

Revamping game night with family is a fantastic way to bond and create lasting memories. By establishing ground rules, encouraging good sportsmanship, keeping score, and creating an engaging environment, you will indeed have a game night to remember. So have fun and enjoy making new memories with loved ones.

Making It Memorable

Family game nights create opportunities for families to have fun, bond, and create lasting memories. But, whether you're a family of four or a more prolific family, there is a way to make the game night even more special. In this section, you'll find ideas on revamping game night to make it more memorable.

Creating Traditions

Start by creating a tradition. A tradition instills a sense of belonging and provides a sense of continuity in our unpredictable world. You might think you don't have any family traditions, but you'll be surprised at how many you already have. For example, does your family always eat nachos during game night? Do you have a specific game that everyone loves to play? These little things, when done consistently, become traditions. Consider incorporating new things, such as having everyone wear matching team shirts or having a themed game night.

Sharing Stories and Playing Music

Playing music and sharing stories are great ways to make the game night memorable. You can create a playlist of your family's favorite songs during game night. This will bring back memories and create new ones. For stories, each family member can share a fun or interesting story. This activity can create good laughter and improve communication skills.

Celebrating Victories

Whenever someone wins a game, celebrate their victory. You can create a team cheer or have everyone give high-fives to the winning team. Celebrating successes generates a positive atmosphere and makes everyone feel good about themselves. Adding prizes or rewards to game night can make it even more fun. Get creative with your tips. They don't have to be expensive.

Taking Photos/Videos

Lastly, take lots of photos and videos. These are great memories that you can have forever. You can print them out and put them into albums or make a family game night scrapbook. Then, years later, you can look back at those memories and reminisce about the good times. The videos can also be shared with relatives and friends who couldn't make it to game night.

Making game night more memorable is all about having fun and being creative. With the tips set out, you can ensure that game night is an experience your family will never forget. The game night should be enjoyable and stress-free, so remember to take lots of breaks and stay positive. Most of all, appreciate the time you have with your family and enjoy the moment.

Chapter 6: Cooking and Baking as a Family

One way to bond with your family is by cooking and baking together. In today's fast-paced world, it's getting more and more difficult to carve out precious moments where you can connect, and as everyone has to eat, cooking together is ideal. In addition, it's an excellent way to cultivate a love for food and the art of cooking. There's something magical about combining different ingredients, flavors, and textures to create something delectable. Whether teaching your kids how to make cookies or whipping up a delicious meal for dinner, cooking and baking as a family is a bonding experience everyone will cherish forever.

This chapter will explore five activities and recipes to strengthen family connections. From creating a family recipe book to making cupcakes, these activities will inspire creativity and bring out the best in each family member. With age-appropriate tasks and safety precautions, you can ensure everyone is having a good time while learning, exploring, and enjoying a delicious meal!

Activity 56: Create a Family Recipe Book

Creating a family recipe book can bring back childhood memories.
https://unsplash.com/photos/0S2rRstB_9M

Food is an essential part of every family. We all have that one recipe that has been passed down from generation to generation, and even when we grow up and start our own families, we still hold on to these family recipes. The taste of traditional dishes always brings back memories of our childhood, family get-togethers, and holidays. That's why creating a family recipe book is an excellent idea to keep these delicious treasures safe for generations.

Materials Needed:

- Recipe Collection: Gather all your family's cherished handwritten and printed recipes.
- Blank Recipe Book or Binder: Choose a durable book or binder with enough pages to accommodate all the recipes.

- Dividers or Tabs: Use these to categorize recipes, such as appetizers, main dishes, desserts, etc.
- Recipe Cards: If you prefer a more interactive approach, use blank recipe cards for handwritten entries.
- Pens, Markers, and Art Supplies: These will come in handy if you want to add personal touches and decorations.
- Scanners or Photocopiers: These can be useful for digitizing old handwritten recipes.
- Camera or Smartphone: For capturing appetizing photos of the prepared dishes.
- Family Members' Input: Reach out to family members for additional recipes and anecdotes.
- Computer and Printer: If you're planning to include digital recipes or typed stories.

Step-by-Step Instructions:

1. Recipe Gathering: Collect recipes from family members. This can include traditional favorites, special occasion dishes, and those with heartwarming stories.
2. Sort and Categorize: Organize recipes into categories like breakfast, appetizers, main courses, desserts, and drinks. Use dividers or tabs to separate these sections.
3. Record Family Stories: Alongside each recipe, add a brief backstory or memory associated with it. This adds a personal touch and makes the book even more special.
4. Personalize the Pages: If using a blank recipe book or binder, write or type the recipes on the pages. If using recipe cards, encourage family members to handwrite their contributions.
5. Include Photographs: Add pictures of the finished dishes for visual appeal. These photos can evoke fond memories and make the book more engaging.
6. Decorate Creatively: If desired, use markers, stickers, or art supplies to decorate the pages. You can create a unified theme or let each recipe have its unique design.
7. Digitize and Preserve: Consider scanning or photocopying handwritten recipes to ensure their preservation. You can add digital versions to the book or store them separately.
8. Family Contributions: Invite family members to contribute their recipes and memories, making the book a collaborative effort.
9. Test and Adapt: Prepare a few recipes from the book to ensure accuracy and taste. Adjust instructions if needed and note any variations.

Benefits:

- Preservation of Traditions: Family recipes carry the essence of generations and cultures, preserving them for years.
- Legacy for Generations: A recipe book is a tangible legacy to pass on to future generations, ensuring they can savor the flavors of the past.

Creating a family recipe book is like crafting a culinary tapestry that weaves together flavors, memories, and stories. As you compile these treasured recipes, you're not just creating a cookbook. You're preserving a piece of your family's history and sharing a timeless gift with future generations. From the handwritten notes of a beloved grandparent to the carefully documented secrets of a special dish, your family recipe book will become a cherished heirloom that nourishes the body and soul, one recipe at a time.

Themed Dinner Nights

Cooking and baking with your family is a way to bond and create memories and an opportunity to teach essential life skills like organization, patience, and teamwork. Hosting themed dinner nights is a fun way to make the experience even more enjoyable. It lets you get creative in the kitchen and is a fun activity for the whole family. This section discusses different themed dinner night ideas and how to make the experience successful.

Activity 57: Taco Night

This theme is perfect for any family who loves Mexican food. You could set up a toppings bar with different meats, beans, and veggies and let everyone build their own tacos. You can even make homemade tortillas and salsa to take the meal to the next level. Remember to create a festive atmosphere by playing some lively Latin music and decorating the table with sombreros and colorful tablecloths.

Activity 58: Italian Night

Who doesn't love a big, hearty bowl of pasta? You can get creative with different sauces and pasta shapes with Italian Night. You can also make appetizers like bruschetta or Caprese salad. To make it even more fun, play some Italian tunes and have everyone dress up in red, white, and green.

Activity 59: Breakfast Dinner Night

Breakfast for dinner? Yes, please! This theme is perfect for any family who loves brunch. You can make sweet dishes like pancakes or waffles – or savory dishes like omelets. For an added touch, decorate the table with flowers and use fancy plates and silverware.

Activity 60: BBQ Night

This theme is perfect for any summertime gathering. Fire up the grill and make burgers, hotdogs, and ribs. You can also make sides like mac and cheese or baked beans. Set up some lawn games like cornhole or frisbee to make it even more fun.

Activity 61: Japanese Night

Sushi, anyone? Japanese Night is perfect for families that love Asian cuisine. You can make sushi rolls, dumplings, and rice bowls. For an added touch, decorate the table with chopsticks and paper lanterns. You can also play some traditional Japanese music to set the mood.

Themed dinner nights are a fun and creative way to bond with your family in the kitchen. With so many different themes, there is something for every family's taste. Remember to get the whole family involved in the planning process to make it even more of a bonding experience. Remember to take pictures and create lasting memories!

Activity 62: Bake and Decorate Desserts

Sharing a common interest like cooking and baking can bring your family together and create an enjoyable way to connect. One fun activity you can include in your family's cooking and baking routine is decorating desserts. Not only is it a great way to spend time together, but it also allows for creativity and personal expression. Here's everything you need to know for baking and decorating desserts with your family.

Materials Needed:

- Baking Ingredients: Flour, sugar, eggs, butter, and any specific ingredients for your chosen dessert.
- Baking Tools: Mixing bowls, measuring cups and spoons, electric mixer, spatulas, baking pans, and parchment paper.
- Decorating Supplies: Frosting, icing bags and tips, food coloring, sprinkles, edible glitter, chocolate chips, fruit slices, and other decorative items.
- Aprons and Towels: Keep things mess-free and comfortable by donning aprons and having towels on hand.
- Recipe: Choose a dessert recipe that suits your family's preferences and skill level.
- Camera: Capture the creative process and the final masterpiece.

Step-by-Step Instructions:

1. Select a Recipe: Choose a dessert recipe that suits your family's taste and skill level. It could be cookies, cupcakes, a cake, or even a more intricate pastry.
2. Gather Ingredients: Collect all the necessary ingredients and tools to ensure a smooth baking process.
3. Preparation: Preheat the oven as per the recipe instructions. Assemble all the ingredients and utensils on the countertop for easy access.
4. Mix and Bake: Involve everyone in measuring and mixing the ingredients according to the recipe. Let each family member take turns to contribute.
5. Baking Time: Pop the dessert into the oven and use this time to discuss the decorating plans or engage in a fun kitchen-related game.
6. Cooling Phase: Once the dessert is baked, allow it to cool completely before moving on to decorating.
7. Decorating Delights: Set up a decorating station with an array of frosting, icing colors, sprinkles, and other decorative items. Let each family member's creativity shine as they adorn the desserts.
8. Themed Creations: Consider choosing a theme for your dessert decorations. It could be seasonal (like Halloween or Christmas), based on a favorite movie or book, or just a burst of colorful creativity.

Benefits:

- Creativity: Decorating desserts lets each family member express their unique creativity and style.

- Life Skills: Children learn valuable kitchen skills, from measuring ingredients to mastering basic techniques.

By including decorating desserts as part of your cooking routine, your family can enjoy creativity and personal expression while learning valuable skills. Remember to have fun, be patient with one another, and celebrate your successes together. Creating meaningful memories in the kitchen is a gift your family will cherish for years.

Activity 63: DIY Pizza Bars

Imagine a scene where your family gathers around a table filled with a colorful array of toppings, sauce, cheese, and dough. The air is filled with laughter and anticipation as each family member embarks on a culinary adventure to design their perfect pizza. DIY pizza bars offer a delightful experience along with a chance for creativity and bonding.

Materials Needed:
- Pizza Dough: Pre-made or homemade dough, depending on your preference.
- Sauce Selection: Tomato sauce, pesto, white sauce, or any other preferred base.
- Cheese Variety: Mozzarella, cheddar, parmesan, and more.
- Toppings Galore: A variety of vegetables (bell peppers, mushrooms, onions, olives, etc.), meats (pepperoni, sausage, ham, etc.), and herbs (basil, oregano, etc.).
- Cooking Tools: Baking sheets or pizza stones, rolling pin, pizza cutter, spatula.
- Dipping Sauces: Optional, but adding a selection of dipping sauces like marinara, garlic butter, or ranch can enhance the experience.
- Aprons and Chef Hats: To create a festive and engaging atmosphere.

Step-by-Step Instructions:
1. Preparation Stage: Set up a spacious area where everyone can access the toppings easily. Lay out all the ingredients, sauces, and cheese in separate bowls.
2. Roll Out the Dough: If using pre-made dough, follow the package instructions for rolling it out. If making your own, get ready-rolled dough or prepare it in advance.
3. Sauce Spreading: Provide spoons for each family member to spread their choice of sauce over their pizza base. Remind them that the sauce is the canvas upon which they'll build their masterpiece.
4. Cheese Adventure: Let the cheese layer commence! Encourage everyone to sprinkle their preferred cheese generously over their sauced dough.
5. Top It Off: This is where the creativity shines. Each family member can design their pizza with an assortment of toppings. From classic combinations to adventurous creations, let imaginations run wild.
6. Into the Oven: Once the pizzas are dressed to perfection, transfer them onto baking sheets or pizza stones and place them in a preheated oven. Follow the dough's baking instructions for a golden crust.
7. Dip and Delight: While the pizzas bake, set out an array of dipping sauces to accompany the final product.

Benefits:
- Customization: Everyone gets to design their pizza according to their taste and preferences.
- Collaboration: Working together in the kitchen fosters teamwork and a shared accomplishment.

Creating a DIY pizza bar turns an ordinary meal into an exciting culinary adventure. It's a unique opportunity to blend flavors, experiment with toppings, and, most importantly, bond as a family over a shared activity. From shaping the dough to selecting toppings and watching the pizzas bake, each step is an expression of creativity and unity!

Activity 64: Fun Cupcakes

Making cupcakes as a family can be an enjoyable experience.
Photo by Brooke Lark on Unsplash

In the realm of sweet treats, cupcakes hold a special place. The allure of these miniature cakes lies in their delectable taste and the joy of baking them together as a family. Whether you're a seasoned baker or just starting your culinary journey, creating cupcakes can transform an ordinary afternoon into a delightful adventure.

Materials Needed:
- Cupcake Ingredients: Flour, sugar, eggs, butter, baking powder, vanilla extract, milk, and any additional flavors or mix-ins.
- Mixing Bowls and Utensils: Bowls, spoons, measuring cups, and a hand mixer for efficient mixing.

- Cupcake Liners: Colorful and festive cupcake liners to add flair to your creations.
- Baking Pans: Use a cupcake or muffin tin to hold the batter while baking.
- Frosting and Decorations: Various types of frosting (buttercream, cream cheese, etc.), food coloring, piping bags, and decorating tips.
- Toppings: Sprinkles, chocolate chips, fruit, edible glitter, and any other creative toppings your family enjoys.
- Aprons and Oven Mitts: For a touch of baking style and safety.

Step-by-Step Instructions:

1. Gather Ingredients: Assemble all the necessary ingredients and materials in a clean and organized workspace. Put on your aprons and get ready to dive into the baking adventure.
2. Mix the Batter: Depending on your chosen recipe, combine the dry and wet ingredients in separate bowls. Then, slowly incorporate the wet mixture into the dry ingredients until you have a smooth batter.
3. Line the Pans: Place colorful cupcake liners in the cupcake/muffin tins. This adds a decorative touch and makes it easier to remove the cupcakes after baking.
4. Fill the Liners: Using a spoon or ice cream scoop, fill each cupcake liner with the batter until they're about two-thirds full. This allows room for the cupcakes to rise.
5. Bake to Perfection: Preheat your oven to the temperature specified in your recipe. Carefully place the cupcake pans in the oven and bake according to the recipe's instructions.
6. Cool and Frost: Once the cupcakes are baked and golden, remove them from the oven and let them cool completely on a wire rack. While waiting, prepare your choice of frosting.
7. Decorate with Flair: This is where the fun truly begins. Set up a decorating station with an assortment of frostings, toppings, and decorations. Let each family member unleash their creativity and decorate their cupcakes as they please.

Benefits:

- Bonding Time: Baking as a family fosters connection and shared experiences.
- Skill Development: Children learn basic baking techniques and kitchen safety.

Baking fun cupcakes together is more than a culinary activity. It's a delightful way to nurture family bonds and create lasting memories. From mixing ingredients to artistic decoration, every step becomes an opportunity to laugh, learn, and express creativity!

This chapter discussed five easy ways to make cooking and baking a happy, bonding family time. A unique recipe accompanies each activity so you can create something special together. From creating a family recipe book to baking and decorating cupcakes, these activities will bring your family closer together and create lasting memories.

Chapter 7: Sharing and Creating Stories

Sharing stories with family is a memorable, one-and-only family experience that can bring you closer together and create lasting bonds. Whether it's sharing your personal experiences or creating new stories together, storytelling allows us to connect on a deeper level and better understand each other's perspectives. In addition, it's a chance to step away from the hustle and bustle of daily life and take a moment to reflect, reminisce, and appreciate all that we have accomplished and overcome as a family.

Sharing stories with family can bring you closer together.
https://unsplash.com/photos/c_rnPbSYVFM?utm_source=unsplash&utm_medium=referral&utm_content=creditShareLink

Activity 65: Family Story Circle Sessions

Amidst the whirlwind of our modern lives, where time often slips through our fingers, the essence of family bonding can sometimes fade into the background. However, there exists a timeless tradition that has the power to reignite these connections and create treasured memories: storytelling. Gathering as a family to share stories, whether they're personal anecdotes or snippets from the past, has the magical ability to forge unbreakable bonds.

Materials Needed:

- Comfortable Seating: Arrange a cozy space with ample seating for everyone to sit comfortably.
- Mementos and Photos: Gather photo albums, family heirlooms, and mementos that might spark storytelling.
- Writing Materials: Provide notebooks and pens for those who wish to jot down story ideas.

Step-by-Step Instructions:

1. Set the Mood: Choose a relaxing and distraction-free environment for your Family Story Circle Session. Dim the lights, light some candles, or sit by a crackling fire to create an inviting atmosphere.
2. Create a Safe Space: Emphasize that this is a judgment-free zone. Encourage everyone to be open, honest, and vulnerable while sharing their stories.
3. Rotate Storytellers: Begin with a storyteller, perhaps the eldest or youngest family member, who shares a personal story, memory, or anecdote. After each story, rotate to the next family member.
4. Prompt Ideas: To kick off the session, you can use prompts like "Share a memorable childhood adventure" or "Tell us about a family tradition that warms your heart."
5. Listen and Engage: As each family member shares, listen attentively, offering supportive nods, smiles, and laughter where appropriate.
6. Build Upon Stories: Encourage family members to build upon one another's stories. This collaborative element can lead to unexpected twists and turns.
7. Laughter and Tears: Embrace the full spectrum of emotions, from hearty laughter to poignant tears. These shared feelings create deeper connections.
8. Capture the Moments: If desired, designate someone to jot down highlights or takeaways from each story session.

Benefits:

- Strengthened Bonds: Sharing personal narratives fosters understanding and empathy among family members.
- Cultural Legacy: Passing down family stories preserves your cultural and familial heritage for future generations.

Family Story Circle Sessions transcend generations, cultures, and time, uniting family members in a timeless tradition of connection. Through shared laughter, nostalgic tears, and the exchange of personal narratives, these sessions create an environment where every voice matters.

Activity 66: Memory Sharing and Recording through Interviews

Memories are the threads of your past that shape the fabric of your present and future. These cherished recollections hold the key to understanding who you are, where you come from, and the values that guide you. While the task of preserving these memories might seem daunting, the rewards are immeasurable. The art of memory sharing through intimate interviews with family members is a time-honored method to record and safeguard these invaluable narratives.

Materials Needed:
- Recording Device: Use a digital recorder, smartphone, or video camera to capture interviews.
- Notebook and Pen: Keep a notebook handy for jotting down questions, notes, and insights.
- Comfortable Space: Choose a cozy setting where the interviewee feels relaxed and open.
- Photo Albums and Mementos: Gather photos and mementos that can trigger memories during the interview.

Step-by-Step Instructions:
1. Select Interviewees: Begin by selecting family members you'd like to interview. Consider elders, parents, and other relatives with rich life experiences.
2. Choose a Focus: Decide on the theme or topics you want to explore during the interview. This could include childhood memories, significant life events, family traditions, and personal journeys.
3. Prepare Thoughtful Questions: Craft a list of open-ended questions that encourage storytelling. For example, "Tell me about a cherished family tradition" or "Can you recount a turning point in your life?"
4. Create a Comfortable Environment: Set the stage for a relaxed conversation. Ensure the interviewee is at ease and ready to share.
5. Begin with Warm-Up Questions: Start with light questions to establish rapport and help the interviewee ease into the process.
6. Listen Attentively: Listen actively, allowing the interviewee to lead the conversation. Encourage them to delve deeper into their stories.
7. Use Triggers: Share old photos, mementos, or family heirlooms to spark memories and prompt detailed narratives.
8. Follow the Flow: Let the conversation flow naturally. Your role is to guide and facilitate, not dominate the conversation.
9. Capture Emotions: Encourage the interviewee to express their emotions and feelings. These emotional nuances add depth to the recorded memories.
10. Embrace Silence: Don't be afraid of pauses or silence. Sometimes, the most profound reflections emerge in quiet moments.
11. Summarize and Reflect: At the end of the interview, summarize key points and ask the interviewee if they have any final thoughts to share.

Benefits:
- Emotional Connection: Hearing personal stories fosters emotional connections among family members.
- Legacy of Love: A recorded legacy to be passed down, ensuring the continuity of family narratives.

Through the art of memory sharing and recording interviews, you embark on a journey to unearth the treasures of your family's history. Each story shared is a glimpse into the essence of your family's journey through time. Capturing these narratives is an act of preserving the past for the benefit of the future. As you sit down with family members to unravel their memories, you're creating a legacy and strengthening the bonds that tie your family together!

Activity 67: Collaborative Story-Writing Projects

In a world overflowing with digital distractions, finding meaningful ways to bond as a family is a rewarding challenge. Collaborative story-writing projects unleash your family's collective creativity and weave stronger bonds among its members. This endeavor may appear daunting, but fear not! It's a captivating and innovative approach that promises joy, laughter, and the creation of memorable tales.

Materials Needed:
- Paper and Writing Tools: Stock up on paper, notebooks, or a shared digital document for story writing.
- Imagination and Open Minds: The most essential ingredients for crafting unique narratives.
- Willingness to Share: A spirit of openness and willingness to share ideas and thoughts.

Step-by-Step Instructions:
1. Set the Scene: Gather your family in a cozy and inspiring setting. This could be around the fireplace, in the backyard, or even on a virtual call.
2. Choose a Genre: Decide on a genre for your story. Will it be an adventure, mystery, fantasy, or something unique?
3. Initiate the Story: One person starts the story with a captivating opening sentence. This sets the stage for the tale to unfold.
4. Pass the Pen: Each family member takes turns contributing a sentence or a paragraph to the story. The story evolves with every new addition.
5. Build on Ideas: Embrace the unexpected twists and turns that others bring to the story. Build on their ideas and let the narrative take delightful detours.
6. Character Creation: Introduce characters to the story. Each family member can create and develop a character, complete with personalities and quirks.
7. Conflict and Resolution: Add conflict and obstacles to the story. Discuss as a family how the characters will overcome these challenges.
8. Use Your Senses: Encourage vivid descriptions that appeal to the senses. Transport readers into the story's world through rich imagery.
9. Keep It Flowing: Maintain the flow of the story by seamlessly transitioning from one family member's contribution to another's.

10. Don't Overthink: Embrace spontaneity and creativity. There's no need for perfection because the charm lies in the collaborative process.

11. Closure and Ending: As the story nears its conclusion, work together to craft a satisfying ending that wraps up the narrative.

12. Read Aloud: Once the story is complete, gather around and read the story aloud. Revel in the shared accomplishment and the tale you've woven together.

Benefits:

- Unleashing Creativity: Uncover hidden talents and explore the depths of your family's imagination.
- Shared Achievement: The completed story becomes a tangible reminder of your family's collaboration and creativity.

As you embark on collaborative story-writing projects, you venture into a realm where creativity knows no bounds and family bonds flourish. Each sentence crafted, every character introduced, and every twist added becomes a testament to the unity and shared creativity of your family. So, put aside the screens and remote controls and let your collective imagination guide you through the creation of unforgettable stories.

Activity 68: Fortunately, Unfortunately

Dive into the whimsical world of storytelling with the "Fortunately, Unfortunately" game. This creative activity encourages family members to collaborate on a story filled with unexpected twists and turns.

Step-by-Step Instructions:

1. Gather around: Sit in a circle or around a table where everyone can easily see and hear each other.
2. Start with "Fortunately": The first person begins the story with a sentence that starts with "Fortunately." For example, "Fortunately, the sun was shining brightly on the day of the big adventure."
3. Follow with "Unfortunately": The next person continues the story by adding a sentence that starts with "Unfortunately." For instance, "Unfortunately, a sudden storm cloud appeared out of nowhere."
4. Keep the pattern going: Family members take turns alternating between "fortunately" and "unfortunately" as they build the story. Each new sentence should react to the previous one, continuing the narrative.
5. Embrace the twists: Embrace the unexpected! As the story unfolds, you'll encounter delightful surprises and humorous contradictions.
6. Keep it going: Continue the back-and-forth pattern until you feel like the story has reached a satisfying conclusion.

Benefits:

- Creativity: Participants exercise their creativity by weaving a story together in real time, incorporating each other's contributions.
- Collaboration: Family members work together to create a cohesive narrative, learning to build upon each other's ideas.

"Fortunately, Unfortunately" is an entertaining way to experience storytelling as a dynamic and cooperative endeavor. As each participant adds their unique spin to the story, you'll witness the narrative take unexpected and delightful directions.

Activity 69: Word Association

Explore the depths of your family's imagination as you embark on a word association journey. This game is a fantastic way to weave a collective narrative while building connections between words.

Step-by-Step Instructions:
- Gather around: Sit in a circle or arrange yourselves comfortably so that everyone can hear each other.
- Begin with a word: The first person starts by saying a word aloud. It can be any word that comes to mind.
- Connect the dots: The next person responds with a word that is associated with the previous word. For instance, if the first word was "tree," the next word could be "leaves."
- Keep the chain going: Continue the pattern, with each family member responding to the previous word with a word that makes sense in relation to it.
- Explore tangents: As you progress, the words may take unexpected turns, leading to interesting and amusing associations.
- Avoid repetition: Try not to repeat words that have already been used in the game.

Benefits:
- Creativity: Participants exercise their creativity by quickly thinking of words that are related to the previous word.
- Vocabulary Building: The game encourages the use of a wide range of vocabulary, expanding everyone's word bank.

Word Association is a game that takes your family on a linguistic journey, exploring connections between words and discovering the unexpected paths they can lead to. It's a delightful way to foster creativity, language skills, and collaboration among family members.

Activity 70: Scene Building Improv

Unleash your family's inner actors and create hilarious scenes or scenarios with the "Scene Building Improv" exercise. This activity encourages spontaneous storytelling and provides a platform for endless laughter.

Step-by-Step Instructions:
1. Gather the ensemble: Assemble your family members in a comfortable space where everyone can see and hear each other.
2. Set the stage: Begin by announcing a simple scenario or setting, such as "at a bakery," "lost in the jungle," or "on a spaceship."
3. Choose characters: Each family member takes on a character role for the scene. Feel free to get creative. You can be a chef, an explorer, an alien, a talking animal, or anything your imagination conjures.

4. Start the scene: The scene begins with one family member initiating the interaction based on the scenario and their chosen character.
5. React and respond: As the scene progresses, each family member jumps in with their characters, reacting and responding to what's happening. There's no script. It's all about improvisation and spontaneity.
6. Keep the story alive: Continuously build on the story as characters interact, face challenges, and embark on adventures within the chosen setting.
7. Embrace surprises: Expect the unexpected! The charm of improv lies in the unexpected twists and turns that arise from everyone's contributions.
8. Keep the energy flowing: Encourage everyone to jump in and contribute, ensuring that the scene evolves dynamically.

Benefits:

- Laughter: The unpredictable nature of the activity often leads to hilarious situations and uproarious laughter.
- Communication Skills: Improv enhances communication skills by requiring active listening and effective interaction.

Scene Building Improv is a fantastic way to break the ice, encourage spontaneity, and bring a dose of lightheartedness to family gatherings. Through shared storytelling, you'll create memorable moments full of laughter and imagination.

Storytelling games, improv exercises, and collaborative writing projects are great ways to bring families closer together while fostering creativity, communication, and laughter. By preparing appropriately, establishing clear guidelines, and choosing suitable activities, families can create fun and memorable experiences that will enhance their relationships and strengthen their bonds for years to come.

Chapter 8: Activities for Fitness and Fun

Taking care of your family's health and building solid parent-child connections go hand in hand. As a parent, it's natural to want what's best for your children. It includes promoting healthy habits that will help them thrive physically and mentally. But the importance of fostering a positive relationship with your children often gets overlooked. Connecting with them and genuinely listening to their needs and concerns strengthens your bond and provides a safe space for them to grow and develop.

Benefits of Physical Activity for Families

Living a healthy family lifestyle can profoundly impact both parents and children. Regular physical activity improves our overall physical health, boosts our mood, reduces stress, and helps foster strong relationships with our loved ones. In addition, engaging in fitness activities with your kids shows you are setting an excellent example for them to follow and creating opportunities for parent-child bonding. Whether biking, hiking, or playing a game of catch, these activities offer the perfect opportunity for quality time and meaningful conversations.

Exercising with your children can help you create a strong parent-child bond.
https://www.pexels.com/photo/photo-of-girl-hugging-her-mom-while-doing-yoga-pose-4473612/

Safety and Adaptability Considerations

There's no reason to sacrifice fun and fitness for safety. Family activities that promote both can be the perfect solution. The possibilities are endless, from hiking and biking to outdoor scavenger hunts and backyard yoga sessions. The key is choosing engaging, challenging, enjoyable activities for everyone involved. Here are a few tips:

- Equip everyone with the right gear, such as helmets and proper footwear
- Ensure their safety by familiarizing yourself with the activity you plan to do and any potential hazards
- Allow for adaptability and flexibility so that everyone can participate at their own pace
- Consider the ages and abilities of each family member before choosing an activity

Activity 71: Cosmic Bowling

Transform your living room into a mini-bowling alley with simple materials and a sprinkle of creativity. The pulsating lights, the thumping music, and the satisfying strike of pins flying are a recipe for pure fun. It's a perfect activity for family game nights, birthday parties, or just a fun way to unwind after a long day. Dim the lights, crank up the tunes, and get ready to roll some strikes.

Materials Needed:
- **Bowling Essentials:** Bowling balls (traditional or lightweight), pins (glow-in-the-dark or decorated), or even empty water bottles as makeshift pins.
- **Lighting:** Blacklights, string lights, fairy lights, disco ball (optional) – get creative!
- **Alley Creation (optional):** Cardboard boxes, furniture, blankets, or any materials you can use to create a makeshift bowling lane.
- **Decorations (optional):** Glow sticks, streamers, posters – add some cosmic flair!
- **Music:** Upbeat tunes to set the mood.

Step-by-Step Instructions:
1. **Set the Scene:** Dim the lights or turn them off completely. Drape your chosen lighting around the room, focusing on the bowling area. If you're creating a makeshift lane, use boxes, furniture, or blankets to define the boundaries.
2. **Glow it up:** Decorate with glow sticks, streamers, or posters to create a cosmic ambiance. Encourage everyone to wear neon or glow-in-the-dark clothing for extra fun.
3. **Get Ready to Roll:** Choose your bowling balls and pins. If using water bottles, fill them with water and add glow sticks for an extra touch.
4. **Strike a Pose:** Crank up the music and get ready to bowl! Keep score as usual, or create your fun scoring system with bonus points for strikes or creative throws.
5. **Celebrate the Winners:** Don't forget to award prizes (real or imaginary) to the champions of the night!

Benefits:
- **Budget-friendly:** Save money on expensive bowling alley trips and enjoy the fun at home.

- **Customization:** Tailor the experience to your preferences. Choose your music, and decorations, and even create your unique bowling challenges.
- **Family Bonding:** Create lasting memories and laughter together as you bowl the night away.
- **Indoor Activity:** Perfect for rainy days or when you want to stay cozy indoors.
- **Promotes Physical Activity:** Bowling is a fun way to get some exercise and have a blast.

Ditch the traditional and embrace the cosmic. With a little creativity and these simple steps, you can bring the excitement of cosmic bowling right into your living room. Turn up the music, grab your glow-in-the-dark gear, and get ready for a night of strikes, laughter, and unforgettable memories.

Activity 72: Family Dance Party

Turn up the energy and groove to the beat with a Family Dance Party! This exhilarating activity brings a burst of fun, laughter, and fitness to your living room, all while bonding with your loved ones.

Materials Needed:
- A playlist of upbeat songs
- A clear space in your living room or any suitable area

Step-by-Step Instructions:
1. Set the Mood: Choose a variety of songs that are upbeat and suitable for dancing. Create a playlist that everyone can enjoy, including songs from different genres.
2. Clear the Space: Move furniture or any obstacles to create a safe and open dance floor. Make sure there's enough room for everyone to move freely.
3. Create a Playlist: Use your favorite music streaming platform to create a playlist of songs that make you want to move. Consider including a mix of old and new tunes to cater to different tastes.
4. Dance Styles: Spice things up by incorporating different dance styles into your dance party. You can try Zumba routines, Latin dance moves, hip-hop steps, or even freestyle dancing.
5. Invite Everyone: Gather your family members and let them know it's time for a dance party! Encourage everyone to join in, regardless of their dance experience.
6. Switch Styles: After a few songs, switch to a different dance style. This keeps the energy high and adds variety to the experience.
7. Encourage Participation: If you have family members who might be hesitant to dance, create an inclusive and supportive environment. Emphasize that it's all about having fun and being active.
8. Cool Down: Slow down the tempo and conclude the dance party with a cool-down. Stretch your muscles gently to prevent any post-dance soreness.

Benefits:
- Cardiovascular Workout: Dancing is a fantastic aerobic exercise that boosts heart health and burns calories.
- Coordination and Balance: Dancing improves coordination and balance, enhancing physical skills.

The Family Dance Party is a lively and enjoyable way to stay active while spending quality time together. Let the music guide you as you dance your way to a healthier and happier family.

Activity 73: Family Hiking Adventure

Embark on an invigorating journey with your loved ones through the beauty of nature with a Family Hiking Adventure. Hiking not only offers a fantastic workout but also creates lasting memories and connections.

Materials Needed:
- Comfortable hiking shoes
- Appropriate clothing for the weather
- Backpack with essentials (water, snacks, first aid kit, sunscreen)
- Trail map or GPS device

Step-by-Step Instructions:
1. Choose a Trail: Research hiking trails in your area that are suitable for your family's fitness level and experience. Look for trails with varying difficulty levels and scenic views.
2. Plan Ahead: Check the trail length, elevation gain, and estimated time to complete the hike. Ensure the trail aligns with your family's capabilities.
3. Pack Essentials: Load your backpack with water bottles to stay hydrated, energy-boosting snacks, a basic first aid kit, and sunscreen. Dress in layers to adjust to changing weather conditions.
4. Safety First: Inform someone about your hiking plans and expected return time. Carry a fully charged mobile phone and a trail map or GPS device.
5. Start Early: Begin your hike early in the day to avoid midday heat and crowds. Set a pace that is comfortable for the entire family, taking breaks when needed.
6. Enjoy the Views: Take in the beauty of the outdoors as you hike. Encourage your family to stop and appreciate the scenic spots along the way.
7. Complete the Scavenger Hunt (Optional): If you've created a scavenger hunt, work together to find the items on your checklist. It adds an element of adventure and fun to the hike.
8. Capture Memories: Bring a camera to capture the breathtaking views and precious moments. These photos will serve as cherished mementos of your family's hiking adventure.

Benefits:
- Nature Connection: Hiking allows your family to disconnect from screens and immerse in the natural world.
- Physical Activity: Hiking provides an excellent cardiovascular workout and helps build endurance.

As you lace up your hiking boots and venture onto the trail, you're creating memories, building bonds, and discovering the wonders of the world together as a family.

Activity 74: Family Yoga Session

Indulge in a serene and rejuvenating experience with your family through a Family Yoga Session. This harmonious activity not only fosters physical well-being but also cultivates mindfulness and strengthens the family's connection.

Materials Needed:
- Comfortable clothing suitable for movement
- Yoga mats or soft surface
- Calming music (optional)
- Open minds and positive energy

Step-by-Step Instructions:
1. Choose a Quiet Space: Find a peaceful and clutter-free area in your home or a tranquil spot outdoors where your family can practice yoga without distractions.
2. Set the Mood: Dim the lights and play soft, soothing music to create a serene ambiance for the yoga session.
3. Basic Poses: If your family is new to yoga, start with basic poses, such as Child's Pose, Downward Dog, Cat-Cow, and Mountain Pose.
4. Breathing Awareness: Guide your family in mindful breathing. Inhale deeply through the nose, feeling the breath expand the belly, and exhale slowly through the mouth, releasing tension.
5. Progressive Poses: Gradually introduce more challenging poses as your family gains confidence and flexibility.
6. Partner Poses (Optional): For added fun and connection, try partner yoga poses. Poses like Double Downward Dog or Seated Forward Fold with a partner can deepen the bond among family members.
7. Guided Meditation: After the yoga sequence, guide your family through a brief meditation. Encourage them to focus on their breath, release stress, and find mental clarity.

Benefits:
- Physical Fitness: Yoga promotes flexibility, balance, and strength while being gentle on the body.
- Stress Relief: Mindful movements and deep breathing reduce stress and anxiety.

Through Family Yoga Sessions, you create an oasis of tranquility and unity amidst the busyness of life. As you breathe, stretch, and move together, you're nurturing your family's physical and emotional well-being while forging a deeper bond that radiates harmony.

Activity 75: Family Water Sports Adventure

Dive into the refreshing world of water sports and create unforgettable memories with your family. From the gentle embrace of kayaking to the exhilaration of paddleboarding, water activities offer a fantastic way to stay active and enjoy the great outdoors.

Materials Needed:
- Appropriate swimwear
- Life jackets for safety
- Water sports equipment (kayaks, paddleboards, surfboards)
- Sunscreen and hats
- Water-resistant bags for valuables
- Refreshments and water bottles

Step-by-Step Instructions:
1. Select the Water Activity: Choose a water sport that suits your family's interests and fitness levels. Whether it's swimming, kayaking, paddleboarding, or a combination of activities, ensure everyone is comfortable with the chosen option.
2. Safety First: Before you embark on your water adventure, familiarize yourself with safety guidelines. Make sure everyone wears properly fitting life jackets and is aware of any specific rules or regulations for the chosen water activity.
3. Choose a Location: Find a suitable water body, such as a calm lake, river, or even the ocean if you're experienced and comfortable.
4. Warm-Up and Stretch: Start with a light warm-up to prepare your muscles for the activity. Gently stretch to prevent injuries and promote flexibility.
5. Introduction and Instruction: If trying a new water sport, provide a brief introduction and basic instructions to the family. Cover techniques for staying balanced, paddling, and navigating.
6. Beginner-Friendly: Keep the pace beginner-friendly, especially if some family members are new to the chosen water sport.
7. Explore and Play: Once everyone feels confident, explore the water body together. Engage in playful activities, such as friendly races, team challenges, or simply enjoying the serenity of being on the water.

Benefits:
- Family Bonding: Sharing an outdoor adventure fosters unity and strengthens family bonds.
- Skill Building: Learning a new water sport enhances coordination and self-confidence.

By engaging in water sports as a family, you're embracing the joy of movement while immersing yourselves in the beauty of nature. The gentle waves become a playground of shared laughter and discovery, making every splash a cherished memory.

Activity 76: Family Cycling Adventure

Embrace the thrill of the open road and embark on a family cycling adventure. Biking not only offers a fantastic cardiovascular workout but also presents the perfect opportunity to explore your surroundings and share quality time with your loved ones.

Materials Needed:
- Bicycles for each family member

- Helmets and protective gear
- Comfortable attire and sneakers
- Water bottles and hydration packs
- Maps or GPS devices for navigation
- Bike trailer or child seat for younger riders

Step-by-Step Instructions:
1. Gear Up: Ensure everyone has well-fitted helmets and appropriate attire. Adjust the bikes to match each family member's height and comfort.
2. Choose Your Route: Decide whether you want to explore local trails and bike paths – or venture out for a longer ride. Research scenic routes that cater to your family's skill level.
3. Safety Briefing: Before setting off, review basic bike safety rules. Teach hand signals for turns and remind everyone to stay on designated paths.
4. Warm-Up: Begin with a gentle warm-up to get your muscles ready for the ride. Start with slower pedaling and gradually increase your pace.
5. Mindful Riding: Encourage everyone to ride at a comfortable pace and be mindful of their surroundings. Use the ride as an opportunity to relax and clear your mind.
6. Family Games: Add an element of fun by incorporating family-friendly biking games. Challenge each other to a friendly race or create a scavenger hunt based on items you might encounter during the ride.
7. Rest Stops: Plan rest stops along the route. Use these breaks to stretch, enjoy a snack, and rest before continuing your journey.

Benefits:
- Cardiovascular Workout: Biking provides an excellent cardiovascular exercise that's gentle on the joints.
- Mental Refreshment: Biking in nature offers a mental break from daily routines.

As you pedal together, the wind in your hair becomes a shared sense of freedom, and each mile covered is a testament to your family's unity and determination. Whether you're cycling through urban trails or countryside lanes, the journey itself becomes a cherished memory etched in the pavement.

Activity 77: Family Sports Tournament

Ignite the spirit of healthy competition within your family by organizing a thrilling sports tournament. Whether it's football, basketball, volleyball, or any other sport, a family sports tournament is an exhilarating way to bond, showcase your skills, and create lasting memories.

Materials Needed:
- Sports equipment based on the chosen sport (soccer ball, basketball, volleyball)
- Court or playing area suitable for the sport
- Team jerseys or colored bands to distinguish teams
- Water bottles and hydration stations
- First aid kit for any minor injuries

Step-by-Step Instructions:

1. Choose the Sport: Discuss with your family and select a sport that everyone enjoys and can participate in comfortably. Consider the space available and any safety concerns.
2. Form Teams: Divide the family into teams. To promote camaraderie, mix different ages and skill levels within each team.
3. Set the Rules: Establish clear and age-appropriate rules for the chosen sport. Make sure everyone understands the rules and expectations.
4. Prepare the Venue: Set up the playing area according to the sport's requirements. For example, mark boundaries on a field, set up a basketball hoop, or create a volleyball court.
5. Warm-Up: Begin with a group warm-up to prevent injuries. Incorporate dynamic stretches and light cardio to prepare the muscles for physical activity.
6. Friendly Matches: Organize a series of matches between the teams. Keep the matches light-hearted and fun, emphasizing the spirit of friendly competition.
7. Cheering Squad: Designate some family members as the cheering squad for each team. Encourage positive cheering and sportsmanship.
8. Hydration Breaks: Schedule regular breaks for water and rest. Staying hydrated is essential, especially during physical activities.
9. Team Bonding: Between matches, provide opportunities for teams to strategize, bond, and discuss their game plan.
10. Tournament Finale: After all matches are completed, celebrate with a friendly awards ceremony. Recognize teamwork, sportsmanship, and any outstanding performances.

Benefits:

- Healthy Competition: A sports tournament fosters friendly competition and encourages everyone to give their best.
- Teamwork: Working together in teams promotes collaboration and communication.

As you dive into the heart-pounding matches, every pass, shot, and goal becomes a shared triumph. The laughter, cheers, and even the occasional playful rivalry create a tapestry of memories that will stay with your family long after the tournament ends.

Activity 78: Family Olympics

Bring the spirit of friendly competition and sportsmanship to your family with a mini Olympics. This multi-sport event allows everyone to participate in various challenges and games, fostering teamwork and active fun.

Materials Needed:

- Sports equipment, such as balls, cones, hula hoops, jump ropes, etc.
- Stopwatch or timer
- Prizes or ribbons for winners (optional)

Step-by-Step Instructions:

1. Select Activities: Choose a variety of activities that family members can compete in. These can include relay races, sack races, hula hoop contests, soccer dribbling, and more.

2. Set Up Stations: Arrange different stations for each activity. Ensure there's enough space for each challenge.
3. Demonstrate Activities: Briefly explain each activity and demonstrate how it's done. Make sure everyone understands the rules and objectives.
4. Team Assignments: Divide the family into teams or pairs. Mix up the teams to encourage bonding and collaboration.
5. Rotate and Compete: Assign a specific time for each station. Family members rotate through the stations, competing in the activities and trying to earn points for their team.
6. Tally Points: Keep track of points earned by each team throughout the mini Olympics.
7. Celebrate and Award: At the end of all the activities, gather everyone and announce the winning team. You can award prizes or ribbons to celebrate their achievements.

Benefits:
- Healthy Competition: Friendly competition promotes teamwork, sportsmanship, and a healthy spirit of rivalry.
- Positive Memories: The shared experience of competing and celebrating fosters cherished memories.

As the family engages in a range of athletic challenges, the cheers, laughter, and determination remind everyone that being part of a team, regardless of who wins, is the true victory.

Activity 79: Frizbee Fenzie

Step into the world of outdoor fun with a thrilling game of Frizbee Fenzie. It's an energetic combination of Ultimate Frisbee and tag that guarantees laughter, teamwork, and active enjoyment for the entire family.

Materials Needed:
- Frisbee (multiple if possible)
- Open outdoor spaces like a park or a field
- Cones or markers to designate boundaries

Step-by-Step Instructions:
1. Set the Boundaries: Choose an open outdoor area and mark the boundaries using cones or other markers.
2. Form Teams: Divide your family into two teams. You can assign teams randomly or mix up the ages and abilities for more balance.
3. Understand the Rules: Explain the rules of the game to your family. Frizbee Fenzie is a combination of tag and Ultimate Frisbee, where players aim to catch the frisbee while avoiding being tagged.
4. Start the Game: Begin the game by having one team throw the frisbee to the other team. The receiving team must catch the frisbee to gain control.
5. Pass and Score: The team in control of the frisbee works together to pass it among themselves. The goal is to successfully pass the frisbee to a teammate in the opponent's end zone, scoring a point.

6. Avoid Being Tagged: The other team aims to tag the player with the frisbee. Once tagged, that player must stop moving and pivot on one foot. They can still pass the frisbee to teammates but cannot move.
7. Tagged Players Rejoin: If a tagged player receives a pass from a teammate, they are freed from being tagged and can move again.
8. Interception and Turnover: If a frisbee is not caught by the receiving team or is intercepted by the opposing team, possession changes, and the game continues.
9. Scoring and Winning: Keep track of points for each successful pass leading to a score. The team with the most points at the end of the game wins.

Benefits:
- Strategy and Coordination: Players develop strategies for passing and catching while coordinating their movements.
- Fun and Laughter: The blend of Ultimate Frisbee and tag guarantees laughter and enjoyment for the whole family.

Frizbee Fenzie brings a dash of excitement and an abundance of fun to your family outdoor time. As frisbees soar through the air and players dash around, bonds strengthen, and shared memories are woven into the fabric of your family's journey. So, gear up and unleash the frisbee frenzy!

Activity 80: The Water Balloon Challenge

Get ready to make a splash with the thrilling and refreshing family water balloon challenge. This exhilarating relay game will have your family working together, laughing, and cooling off in the best way possible.

Materials Needed:
- Water balloons (prepare a generous supply)
- Buckets or containers filled with water
- Open outdoor spaces like a yard or park
- Towels and swim gear (because things might get wet!)

Step-by-Step Instructions:
1. Set Up the Game Area: Choose a spacious outdoor area for the water balloon challenge. Lay out the buckets of water and place them at a comfortable distance from each other.
2. Form Teams: Divide your family into teams. You can have two or more teams, depending on the number of participants.
3. Create a Relay Line: Each team lines up behind their designated bucket of water. Make sure there's ample space between the teams to avoid collisions.
4. Fill the Balloons: Have each team member fill a water balloon from their team's bucket. Make sure the balloons are filled to a size that's easy to handle and won't burst too easily.
5. Ready, Set, Go!: Start the challenge by having the first players from each team hold their water balloons. When the game begins, they race towards a designated point and back while carrying the water balloon.

6. Pass the Balloon: Upon returning to their team, the first players pass the water balloon to the second players. The second player then repeats the process, racing with the balloon to the designated point and back.

7. Keep Passing and Racing: The relay continues with each team member taking a turn. As the water balloons are passed and raced with, some might burst, adding an extra element of surprise and excitement.

8. Finish Line and Victory: The relay ends when all team members have completed their turns. The first team to have all members finish the relay wins the water balloon challenge.

Benefits:

- Reflexes and Coordination: Players improve their reflexes and hand-eye coordination as they handle and pass water balloons.
- Outdoor Fun: The game encourages outdoor play and enjoying the sun while staying cool.

The water balloon challenge is a fantastic way to create joyful memories and beat the heat during the summer months. As water balloons soar through the air and laughter fills the atmosphere, the bonds between family members grow stronger. So, put on your swim gear, grab those water balloons, and dive into a world of watery excitement with your loved ones!

Families that play together stay together! Regarding bonding experiences, few things can beat getting active as a family. Whether going for a bike ride, having a picnic in the park, or even a friendly game of soccer, family activities for fitness and fun are a great way to strengthen the bond between family members and promote healthy lifestyles. But why stop at just your own family? Involving other families in these activities expands your social circle and creates opportunities for new friendships and shared memories. So, gather your family and friends, and get ready to have fun while staying fit!

Chapter 9: Traveling Together: Day Trip Ideas

There's nothing quite like going on a day trip with people you love. Traveling together is a beautiful way to create lasting memories and strengthen relationships. When it comes to day trips, the options are endless. You could spend the day exploring a nearby city, hiking through a nearby park, or hitting an amusement park. The best part is that you don't need to plan and book an entire vacation.

Benefits of Shared Family Adventures

Day trips with family can strengthen your bond.
https://www.pexels.com/photo/father-with-little-kid-resting-on-rocky-ground-near-river-in-mountains-3933498/

Spending quality time with family members is essential to a happy and healthy family life. But in our fast-paced world, where everyone juggles work, school, and other commitments, family time often takes a backseat. However, taking on a shared family adventure is a perfect way to bond, create lasting memories, and even learn new things together.

- **Strengthened Bond**: Shared family adventures help create a stronger bond between family members. Participating in an activity together creates an opportunity to create happy memories. Whether it's a hiking trip, trying new foods, or teaming up for a sport, families must work together to overcome challenges, learn new things, and share a joyful experience. These shared experiences make family members feel closer, strengthening the family bond.
- **Educational Value**: Shared family adventures offer a learning opportunity for everyone involved. There's always something new to discover, whether it's learning about nature, history, or different cultures. Families can visit museums and historical sites, take guided tours, or even study a new language together. Learning together helps engender interest, curiosity, and an appreciation for other cultures and ways of life.
- **Cultural Exploration**: Shared family adventures allow for the exploration of different cultures, foods, and traditions. Families who travel to new places can experience the unique customs and practices of people from other regions and countries. For instance, trying traditional dishes, visiting local markets, and attending cultural festivals can expose you and your family to new perspectives and help develop a better understanding of different cultures.
- **Recreational Activities**: Shared family adventures offer a chance to participate in recreational activities like swimming, surfing, hiking, camping, and biking, among others. These activities help promote an active lifestyle, boost physical health, and enhance mental well-being. Participating in outdoor activities also allows family members to unplug from technology and connect with nature, which can be therapeutic.

Simple Trip Ideas and Their Benefits

Are you looking for an affordable family trip close to home that doesn't require much planning? Plenty of simple trip ideas for families can boost your family's happiness, strengthen your relationships, and create special memories without breaking the bank. Here are three trip ideas your whole family will love!

Activity 81: Shopping Outlets

Who doesn't love a shopping trip? Shopping outlets are a go-to for families looking for a fun and exciting outing. It is a great way to spend quality time together, and shopping outlets are often located in scenic areas where you can take a walk and enjoy the local scenery and landscape. As you walk around, you will find items to add to your cart, then enjoy the thought of bagging discounts galore! You can also pack a picnic lunch and enjoy some outdoor fun at a nearby park or take in the local attractions.

Activity 82: Local Zoo/Aquarium

A visit to the zoo or aquarium is always a great trip idea for families. It's both educational and entertaining, and you and your kids will learn new things about the animals and their habitats. A visit to the zoo or aquarium can also allow your child to learn more about conservation and environmental issues. Encourage your child to ask plenty of questions to learn more about the animals they meet. Plus, there is nothing like watching animals in their natural habitats or learning about the under-the-sea creatures that make you appreciate the world beyond your backyard.

Activity 83: Museum Outing

Museum outings are a fantastic way to introduce your children to art, history, and other cultures. Even young children can develop and appreciate their creativity and imagination through museum exhibits. Exposure to different art forms and cultural experiences can encourage children to think outside the box and expand their perspectives. Some museums even offer special events for kids, such as scavenger hunts to engage the younger minds. Why not take your family to discover some of the world's most fascinating exhibitions?

Activity 84: Bike Ride

If the weather is nice, why not take your family on a bike ride? It's an easy way to get everyone outdoors and active while having fun. Plus, it's a great way to explore new places together and share stories along the ride. With some simple research, you will be able to find trails for all levels of cyclists in your area. Bring snacks and plenty of water to keep everyone energized!

Activity 85: Beach Trip

Nothing beats a beach trip for a day of fun in the sun. Pack up some outdoor games, sunscreen, and your beach bag with towels and sandwiches for a perfect day out! The beach is also a great place to practice activities, such as swimming, surfing, and kayaking. And, of course, the beach is a great place to relax and enjoy quality family time.

Activity 86: Local Nature Trails

Hiking with your family is the perfect way to appreciate nature at its best. Find a peaceful spot in your area and get out there to explore the natural wonders of your local environment. It's also an excellent opportunity to engage kids in conversations about wildlife, plants, and trees. Bring along some binoculars for a closer look at the flora and fauna!

Activity 87: Outdoor Movie Night

Enjoy a unique movie night experience with your family by setting up an outdoor theatre. All you need is some popcorn, comfortable seating and blankets to snuggle up in, and a projector or laptop to show the movie of your choice. To make it extra special, set up some lawn chairs around the screen for a more classic cinema feel. For added fun, you could even turn the movie night into a real outdoor movie party and invite friends, family, and neighbors to join in!

Activity 88: Amusement Park

What better way to enjoy the summer than at an amusement park? There are plenty of fun activities for all ages, including roller coasters, bumper cars, and water rides, perfect for a day full of thrills and laughter. Or, if you're looking for something more relaxed, some parks offer mini golfing, Ferris wheels, and carousels for a more laid-back experience. Make sure to pack comfortable clothes and shoes for the day's activities!

Activity 89: Water Park

Beat the summer heat with a trip to the nearest water park! You can plunge into exciting attractions, such as inner tubes, body slides, lazy rivers, wave pools, and so much more. The little ones can even enjoy some of the kiddie slides and pools. There is something for everyone to enjoy! Pack swimsuits, towels, and sunscreen for a fantastic day out in the water.

Activity 90: National Parks

Explore the wonders of nature with your family at a national park. Hiking trails, swimming holes, geysers, canyons, and stunning views are just some of the attractions you can find in national parks. Take your time to appreciate the beauty of nature while learning more about the environment and its creatures. Bring along a camera for some everlasting memories!

Activity 91: Trampoline Park

Bounce off those energy levels with a trip to a trampoline park! With wall-to-wall trampolines, foam pits, and lots of other fun activities, such as dodgeball and basketball, the whole family is sure to have an amazing time. Make sure everyone's wearing comfortable clothing that won't restrict their movements for this fun activity.

Activity 92: Outdoor Concert

Enjoy a night of music and entertainment with your family at an outdoor concert. You can find all sorts of events, such as jazz and blues, country, rock, and more. Choose something for everyone in the family to enjoy! Pack some snacks and comfortable seating to relax while listening to great music under the stars.

Activity 93: Mini Golf

Get out on the golf course with your family and have a friendly competition! Mini golf is great for all ages, from young kids to adults. It's also an excellent way to practice teamwork and sportsmanship while having fun together. Plus, some mini golf courses offer additional activities, such as go-karts or batting cages, for the whole family to enjoy.

Activity 94: Kayaking

Learn the basics of kayaking with your family and explore the waters around you. It's a great way to get out and enjoy quality time together while getting some exercise. Wear life vests, bring plenty of water and snacks, and practice safety guidelines for a fun but safe day out on the water. It's sure to be an adventure you won't forget!

Activity 95: Ziplining

Take your family on an exciting adventure with a zipline tour! You'll be soaring high above the treetops and enjoying spectacular forest views. Wear comfortable clothes, closed-toe shoes, and safety gear for this thrilling activity. It's a great way to get the adrenaline pumping and create lasting memories for everyone.

Activity 96: Rock Climbing

Challenge yourself and your family to a rock climbing adventure! This is a great way to bond, build trust, and have fun while getting some exercise at the same time. If you're new to the activity, there are plenty of indoor rock climbing gyms that offer classes and rentals for beginners. Wear comfortable clothes and appropriate shoes for the activity.

Activity 97: Outdoor Yoga

Get your body moving with some outdoor yoga! All you need is a yoga mat, a peaceful spot outdoors, and your family for a great way to relax while stretching out those muscles. Plus, there are plenty of online classes available if you don't have a yoga instructor handy.

Activity 98: Flashlight Tag

Take the game of tag to the next level with flashlights! Play it indoors or outdoors after dark, adding an element of stealth and excitement. You can even incorporate different challenges like finding hidden clues or completing tasks to add another layer of fun.

Activity 99: Fishing

Spend a day out fishing with the whole family! You can find plenty of lakes, rivers, and streams where you can fish for some of your favorite species, such as trout, bass, catfish, or panfish. Bring the right gear, such as rods, reels, bait, and other necessary equipment for a successful day out on the water.

Activity 100: Nature Walks

Get some fresh air and explore nature with your family on a nature walk. Bring binoculars to spot some birds or look for tracks in the mud. Talk about different plants and trees you find along the way, or take pictures of anything that catches your eye. It's a great way to enjoy the great outdoors and have some quality time together!

Whether your family loves shopping, being outdoors, or learning about history or wildlife, these simple trip ideas can provide endless opportunities for bonding, learning, and exploring together. In addition, they are easy to plan, budget-friendly, and convenient to get out of the house and experience something new.

Day trip planning can be both exciting and overwhelming. But with these practical tips, you can be sure you will make the most of your next-day trip. Remember that travel is about making memories and experiencing new things, so don't let the planning process weigh you down. Instead, stay flexible, prioritize your itinerary, and enjoy the journey as much as the destination. Bon Voyage!

Chapter 10: Celebrating Togetherness: Family Traditions to Cherish

Family traditions are the backbone of togetherness. Celebrating these moments with our loved ones creates a bond that transcends time and distance. Whether gathering around the table for a special meal, coming together for a holiday, or just enjoying a Sunday evening ritual, these traditions make our families unique. They are the threads that weave our individual stories into one cohesive narrative. Whenever we look back on these cherished memories, we are reminded of the love and laughter we shared with those we hold dear.

Family traditions create bonds that last through generations.
https://www.pexels.com/photo/family-sitting-at-table-3807395/

Ultimately, there is something magical about celebrating togetherness and family traditions. They help us connect in profound, meaningful, and unforgettable ways. This chapter explores the importance of family traditions, provides some ideas for customizing celebrations, and offers tips on establishing and maintaining these rituals over time. By the end of this chapter, readers will understand why family traditions matter and be inspired to create meaningful connections.

Exploring the Benefits of Family Traditions

Family traditions have the power to connect us to our heritage, deepen ties, and create lasting memories that shape our lives. Whether it's a celebratory meal, story or games night, or an annual family vacation, these traditions provide a sense of stability and meaning that can support us through life's challenges. By honoring our traditions, we pass down values and beliefs from generation to generation, preserving our cultural identity and reinforcing the importance of community. The beauty of our traditions is that they hold the key to a more prosperous, more fulfilling existence.

Cultivating a Sense of Belonging through Shared Customs

Belonging is a fundamental human need. And nothing makes us feel more connected than shared customs. Whether it's a special ceremony, a yearly tradition, or a daily routine, customs provide comfort, familiarity, and community. They bond us like a family and make us feel part of something bigger than ourselves. By cultivating a sense of belonging through shared customs, we create an environment where everyone feels valued, respected, and supported. Customs shape our identity, define our culture and heritage, and remind us of our roots. They unify us in times of joy and sorrow and create lifetime memories.

Ideas for Celebrating Special Occasions

When celebrating special occasions with family, the possibilities are endless. But if you're looking for fresh ideas to create lasting memories, consider starting a weekly or monthly gratitude jar. This simple yet powerful tradition involves taking a few moments each week or month to reflect on what you're thankful for and writing it down on paper, which is then added to a jar. Then, at the end of the year, you can revisit everything you were grateful for as a family.

An annual family photo shoot is another great way to celebrate special occasions. It gives you a beautiful keepsake to cherish for years to come and an opportunity to get everyone together and create new memories. And, of course, no celebration is complete without food! Consider designating one night each month for a special celebratory dinner, where you can cook a special meal together, dress up, and enjoy each other's company. With these ideas, you will create memorable occasions that your family will treasure for years.

Activity 101: Create and Preserve Family Traditions

Family traditions are the threads that weave the fabric of a close-knit family. They create lasting memories, strengthen bonds, and instill a sense of belonging. If you're looking to establish and maintain meaningful family traditions, follow these steps.

Materials Needed:
- Pen and paper or digital device for note-taking
- A family calendar

Step-by-Step Instructions:
1. Reflect on Values and Interests: Gather your family and engage in a thoughtful discussion about your shared values and interests. What activities or rituals hold significance to all family members?
2. Brainstorm Ideas: Encourage each family member to brainstorm ideas for potential traditions. Consider various occasions, such as weekly routines, holidays, birthdays, or annual vacations.
3. Set a Schedule: Decide on the frequency and timing of your traditions. Will they be daily, weekly, monthly, or annually? Create a family calendar to track them.
4. Choose Activities: Select specific activities or rituals that align with your family's values and interests. These could range from game nights and movie nights to hiking trips or volunteering together.
5. Involve Everyone: Ensure that all family members have a say in the traditions you establish. Their involvement will foster a sense of ownership and enthusiasm.
6. Document Your Traditions: Create a document or journal that outlines the details of each tradition. Include the purpose, activities involved, and any special instructions.
7. Implement and Adapt: Begin implementing your chosen traditions and stick to your schedule. Be open to adaptations or improvements as you gain experience.
8. Pass It On: Encourage the passing down of traditions from one generation to the next. This ensures the continuity and preservation of your family's legacy.

Benefits:
- Cherished Memories: Traditions lead to cherished memories that can be revisited and shared over the years.
- Legacy Building: Traditions become part of your family's legacy, connecting generations.

Remember that family traditions should be flexible and adaptable to changing circumstances. They should evolve as your family grows and matures. By establishing and maintaining traditions that reflect your family's uniqueness, you'll create a strong bond that will endure through the generations. So, gather your family and start building traditions that will be cherished for a lifetime.

There's something extraordinary about the power of family traditions. From passing down secret recipes and putting up holiday decorations to taking annual vacations and attending milestone events, these rituals create a bond that transcends time and distance. They allow us to connect with our loved ones in a way that feels both familiar and profound. And what's even more incredible is that the power of family traditions extends far beyond our immediate family members. When we share these customs with our communities and cultural groups, we strengthen our bonds. It's beautiful to be part of something bigger than ourselves. Family traditions provide us with that sense of connection. So, honor these unique customs and embrace their power to bring us closer together.

Conclusion

Spending quality time together is vital to building strong bonds and creating lasting memories as a family. You can do countless indoor or outdoor activities together, regardless of your interests or age. There's something for everyone, from hiking and camping to board games and movie nights. You can even turn mundane tasks like cooking or cleaning into fun family bonding time by involving everyone and turning it into a friendly competition. The possibilities are endless, and the benefits are priceless. You will create beautiful memories and strengthen your relationships, improve communication, and learn new things about each other.

In today's digital age, it's easy to lose sight of the importance of bonding with our loved ones. Screens have become our primary source of entertainment, but they seldom provide the meaningful experiences we need to forge strong connections. That's why now, it's more crucial than ever to find screen-free activities and outdoor adventures to unite families.

This guide covered some of the best ways to spend quality time with your family indoors, outdoors, and even on day trips. Whether hiking through the mountains, playing board games, or simply spending time in nature, these experiences create lasting memories that you and your loved ones will treasure for years to come. By building these bonds, we strengthen our relationships and develop a foundation of trust that can withstand the trials of daily life.

Traveling with family is an incredible opportunity to create unforgettable memories and strengthen the ties of togetherness. This guide also provided some day trip ideas that allow you to explore the world around you and create incredible memories with your loved ones. From hikes to camping trips, day trips are an excellent way to explore new destinations, immerse yourselves in different cultures, and share fascinating experiences. The possibilities are endless, whether it's a scenic drive along the coast, visiting a historical site, or hiking up a mountain trail.

However, the journey itself is just as important as the destination. To enhance the experience, consider creating family traditions you can cherish for years. It could be a song you sing together, a game you play in the car, or a particular food you always eat on the way. Whatever it is, these little yet meaningful traditions can bring you closer and make your travels more memorable. So, pack your bags, hit the road, and celebrate the joy of togetherness with your loved ones.

Check out another book in the series

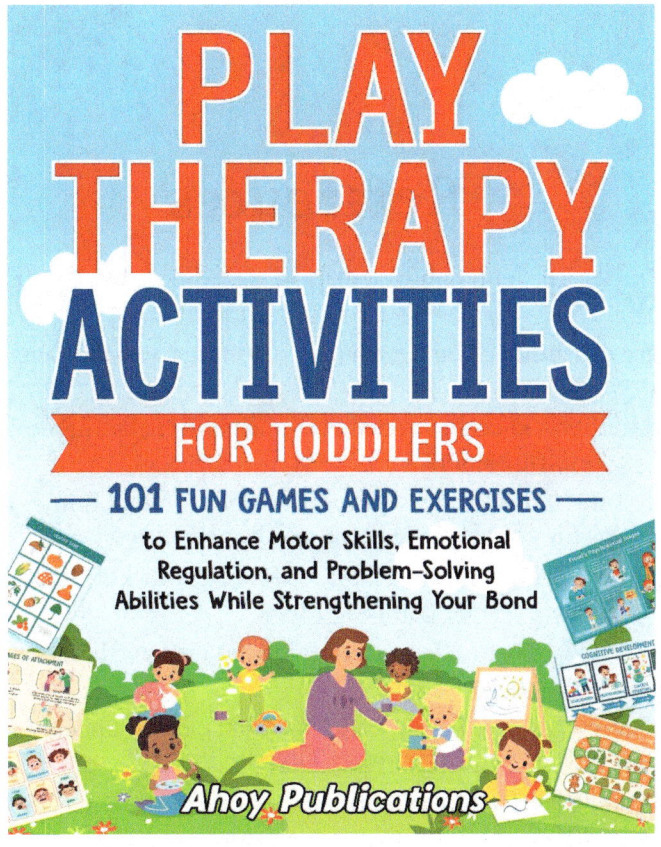

References

Bledsoe, J. (2014, January 3). 101-weekend family activity ideas. All Pro Dad. https://www.allprodad.com/101-weekend-family-activity-ideas/

Daniel, P. (2017). Importance of Family Bonding, 6 Family Bonding activities and games at home | ParentCircle. https://www.parentcircle.com/importance-of-family-bonding-activities-and-games/article

Eatough, E. (n.d.). 20 family tradition ideas to strengthen bonds and make memories. Betterup.com. https://www.betterup.com/blog/family-traditions

Hochswender, C. (2015, July 14). 20 fun family weekend activities to do at home. Parents. https://www.parents.com/fun/activities/outdoor/weekend-family-activities/

Schuman, C. (2015, July 14). 10 unique family activities to do with your kids. Parents. https://www.parents.com/fun/activities/unique-family-activities/

Stephanie. (2022, March 2). Why family bonding is more important now than ever before. Let's Roam Explorer. https://www.letsroam.com/explorer/family-bonding/

Thakur, S. (2020, July 7). 10 ways to create family bonding and its importance. MomJunction. https://www.momjunction.com/articles/family-bonding_00633863/

Today's Parent. (2020, November 18). 87 fun things to do at home— avoid that coronavirus cabin fever - Today's Parent. Today's Parent: SJC Media. https://www.todaysparent.com/family/activities/fun-things-to-do-at-home/

Witmer, D. (2008, September 24). How to strengthen family bonds. Verywell Family. https://www.verywellfamily.com/how-to-strengthen-your-familys-bond-ten-tips-2609591